Table of Contents

TABLES

Introduction

In a recent *New York Times* article, Thomas Friedman argues that four major pillars of the global system are coming unstuck at once. Specifically, he points to the revolutions in the Arab world, the European Union and American debt crisis, and China's unsustainable growth model. He argues that the U.S. is having difficulty just dealing with one of these situations, let alone all four simultaneously.[1] Although the strategic challenges faced by the U.S. may not be as dire as Friedman predicts, the recent Arab revolutions in North Africa are cause for concern. Western leaders are hopeful a desire for Western democracy is the impetus behind Arab unrest. The Obama administration sees the Arab revolutions as a historic opportunity for the region to transition to inclusive democratic societies and economies. In a joint letter the U.S. Secretary of State and Secretary of the Treasury stated, "We share a compelling interest in seeing the transitions in Egypt and Tunisia succeed and become models for the region."[2] However, as events transpire the Arab revolutions generally have brought Islamist governments to power, presenting more strategic challenges for U.S. policy makers.

The recent revolutionary events in Egypt present an ideal case study for examining these challenges. Middle East and North Africa (MENA) scholar Paul Rivlin points out that Egypt is a political and cultural leader; therefore, it acts as a weathervane for the region.[3] Egypt's success or failure concerns both the region and the U.S. The current revolutionary environment in Egypt shares some similarities to the revolutionary environment of the 1950s. Economic stagnation,

---

[1] Thomas L Friedman, "All Together Now" *The New York Times*, August 27, 2011. http://www.nytimes.com/2011/08/28/opinion/sunday/friedman-all-together-now html (accessed October 5, 2011).

[2] Clinton, Hillary Rodham, and Timothy F. Geithner. "Letter to G8 Ministers on Supporting Arab Spring" *U.S. Department of State,* May 25, 2011. http://translations.state.gov/st/english/texttrans/2011/05/20110525104312su0.936134.html (accessed November 27, 2011).

[3] Paul Rivlin, *Arab Economies in the Twenty-First Century* (New York: Cambridge University Press, 2009), 95.

political corruption, an embittered younger generation, and an unpopular great power relationship marked both periods. Sixty years ago, Lieutenant Colonel Gamal Nasser led a revolutionary takeover of the Egyptian monarchy and established a nationalist military dictatorship. More recently, a youthful population protesting poor economic conditions and the authoritarian military-backed regime ushered in a Muslim Brotherhood led government. One result of the 1952 revolution was the nationalization and closure of the Suez Canal in 1956. Western powers launched an unsuccessful military intervention to protect this strategic asset. Similar to sixty years ago, today there is potential for violent confrontation. What is the probability for renewed conflict in the Sinai region in light of Egypt's recent revolution? This monograph will provide insight on that principal question.

Many complex political, economic, social, and military factors influence the current revolutionary environment in Egypt. This makes it difficult to predict what its future holds. Ideally, Egypt will form a stable government that represents Islamist, military and liberal democratic interests and remain at peace with its neighbors. On the other hand, the current revolutionary environment in Egypt may lead to a new Suez style crisis. No matter what happens, if they want to stay in power, Egypt's new leaders will need to address the pressing economic and social demands of the young revolutionary population. Even with an elected civilian government, Egyptian military leaders will fight to retain their international relationships and domestic economic interests. A strong Islamist regime that withdraws from the West would be the worst-case scenario for U.S. interests.

Since it opened in the 1869, the Suez Canal has been a strategic shipping lane. It was economically critical to the British Empire, and it continues to handle 14 percent of global trade, including 3.8 million barrels of oil per day.[4] However, America's strategic relationship with Egypt is about more than economic access. Losing this strategic relationship and access through the Sinai would be a disaster. It would damage U.S. capabilities to mobilize forces to contain Iran and would weaken the overall U.S. defense strategy in the Middle East.[5] Major instability in the Sinai region could threaten traffic through the Suez Canal and seriously affect U.S. interests.

The Muslim Brotherhood will play a major role in the new Egyptian government. The modern image cultivated by the Brotherhood is one of peaceful cooperation and democracy. However, under the surface of this moderate image, anti-Israel, anti-Western, and pro-Caliphate rhetoric continues to drive its faithful followers. A plausible scenario might have the new Islamist Egyptian government consolidate control in Cairo and withdraw from the Camp David Accords. It could also use the Suez Canal as a political and economic tool to make demands on the international community and threaten U.S. interests just as Nasser did in the mid-1950s. This could lead to international military action in the Sinai region to maintain the Suez passageway and prevent an Egyptian-Israeli war.

Some researchers argue that even with a Muslim Brotherhood government, Egypt will maintain good relations with the West. Andrew Terrill, of the U.S. Army's Strategic Studies Institute, reasons that economically challenged Egypt would have difficulty surviving without Western investment, economic aid, and tourism. He concludes that although a more enhanced and independent regional role for Cairo would make U.S.-Egyptian cooperation more difficult, the new government would make substantial efforts to maintain good relations with the West. Terrill goes on to argue that even with political Islam being the mainstream in Egypt, its military leaders

---

[4] Jean-Paul Rodrigue, "Straits, Passages and Chokepoints: A Maritime Geostrategy of Petroleum Distribution" *Erudit,* December 2004. http://www.erudit.org/revue/cgq/2004/v48/n135/011797ar.html?lang=en (accessed April 26, 2012).

[5] David Wood, "At Risk in Egypt's Turmoil: U.S. Military Access to the Middle East" *Politics Daily,* 2011. http://www.politicsdaily.com/2011/02/05/at-risk-in-egypts-turmoil-u-s-military-access-to-the-middle-e/ (accessed September 6, 2012). James Philips is a Senior Middle East researcher at the Heritage Foundation in Washington D.C.

would not allow violent Islamists to operate freely and they would continue to assist U.S. counter-terrorism efforts.[6] Although Egypt's new leaders are reaching out to Iran and Gaza's Hamas Party, researcher Susan Vogelsang argues that in the short-term Egypt's new government will adhere to the Camp David accords to continue receiving U.S. aid. She believes the deep-rooted U.S.-Egyptian political and security alliance will keep pragmatic Islamist leaders in the American camp.[7] Terrill and Vogelsang's arguments assume that Egypt's new Islamist leaders will place Western economic development ahead of the deeper-rooted anti-Israeli, pro-Caliphate passions of the Islamist faithful. The narrative that a Brotherhood-led Egyptian government could eventually spearhead a regional anti-Western Islamist revival is also plausible. No matter what direction Egypt takes in the future, policy makers and military planners must understand the country's complex political, economic, social, and military variables to manage the relationship successfully.

Methodology

To assess the potential for a new Sinai crisis this study will compare the Egyptian revolution and Suez crisis of the 1950s with the current revolutionary environment in Egypt. The study will analyze the two revolutionary environments across the range of political, economic, social, and military variables. The purpose is to provide leaders and policy makers with a deeper understanding of the possibilities for and implications of a future crisis in the Sinai region. Specifically, the study will explore the following questions: Do the lessons from the 1950s have bearing on today's events? What key environmental factors must strategic and operational

---

[6] W. Andrew Terrill, *The Arab Spring and the Future of U.S. Interests and Cooperative Security in the Arab World,* Opinion Editorial (Carlisle, PA: Strategic Studies Institute, United States Army War College, August 2011), 12-13.

[7] Susan S. Vogelsang, *U.S.-Egypt Security Cooperation after Egypt's January 2011 Revolution,* Monograph (Fort Leavenworth, KS: School of Advanced Military Studies, United States Army Command and General Staff College, 2011), 64.

planners consider before applying military force in the region? Using case study analysis and synthesis, this study attempts to shed light on these questions.

The present revolutionary episode in Egypt is still unfolding. This study's conclusions are subject to refinement as new information becomes available and decision makers ultimately chose Egypt's future course. Although it may be presumptuous to speculate about consequences so soon after an event, Yale historian John Lewis Gaddis notes, "an incomplete map is better than no map at all".[8] This monograph provides a better understanding of Egypt's recent revolutionary past and present, while trying to anticipate its future.

The 1950s Revolutionary Environment in Egypt

On July 23, 1952, a small group of mid-grade Egyptian Army officers known as the Free Officers took power by coup. Over the course of the next four years, Nasser gradually consolidated power and turned the Free Officer coup into a revolutionary pan-Arab nationalist movement. In 1956, Nasser exploited regional and global tensions to nationalize the Suez Canal and deliver a diplomatic defeat to the West and Israel, making him an Arab hero in the struggle against colonialism and Zionism. A complex web of political, economic, social, and military variables set the environment that gave rise to Nasser in the 1950s.

The Political Environment

A general sentiment of political disillusionment pervaded pre-revolutionary Egypt due to the instability and inefficacy of its dysfunctional parliamentary system. In July 1951, a newspaper editor described Egypt as a "country of failure" due to corrupt and ineffective political leaders.[9] Spurred by nationalist uprisings after World War I, the British established Egypt's parliamentary

---

[8] John Lewis Gaddis, *Surprise, Security, and the American Experience* (Cambridge: Harvard University Press, 2004), 5.

[9] Joel Gordon, *Nasser's Blessed Movement: Egypt's Free Officers and the July Revolution* (Oxford: Oxford University Press, 1992), 25.

system as a constitutional monarchy in the 1920s. This was a prelude to greater independence from the British in 1936. From 1936 to 1952, King Farouk ruled Egypt. Corruption, pleasure seeking, and infighting typified his reign with a parliament that consisted mainly of professionals and landed aristocrats from the Wafd Party. The Islamist Muslim Brotherhood and a mix of communist parties also competed for influence.[10] Egypt's weak constitution gave excessive powers to the monarch. The king could dismiss cabinets, dissolve parliaments, and appoint and unseat prime ministers. King Farouk often chose unpopular, unelectable, and undemocratic ministers from small minority parties, showing his intolerance for a liberal democratic process.[11] Egypt's weak constitution and competing foreign and national interests doomed the parliamentary order.

The Wafd party represented the liberal democratic tradition in Egypt. Corruption between the Wafd party and the King was commonplace. Three generations with varying interests made up the Wafd party. The old guard were the Pashas, older gentlemen, professionals, and landed aristocracy. They failed to appreciate the danger of the growing disparity between the haves and have-nots in Egypt. The second generation were in their mid to late forties and formed the parliamentary power base. They were impatient for the old guard to relinquish power. The third generation of young professionals and students were the most reform minded and liberally progressive.[12] The Wafd party saw itself as a defender of the constitution against antidemocratic behavior. It represented the landed middle class as well as commercial and professional urban elites.[13] Corruption, rivalry, and polarized ideology between young and old prevented the Wafd party from effectively confronting the Free Officers after July 1952.

---

[10] Ibid., 14-27.

[11] Selma Botman, *Egypt from Independence to Revolution, 1919-1952* (Syracuse: Syracuse University Press, 1991), 5.

[12] Gordon, *Nasser's Blessed Movement*, 22-24.

[13] Botman, *Egypt from Independence to Revolution*, 31.

6

The Muslim Brotherhood in the 1940s and 50s was an anti-establishment Islamist party. Its leader, Hassan al-Banna, advocated a political order rooted in Islamic principles and Egyptian nationalism. The Brotherhood also formed a secret paramilitary organization and infiltrated its members into academic, labor, and government institutions. In December 1948, the paramilitary arm of the Brotherhood assassinated Prime Minister Nuqrashi after he outlawed the organization. The new Prime Minister ruled by martial law to suppress the Brotherhood. In February 1949, the government killed al-Banna in retaliation.[14] The Brotherhood lacked cohesiveness after al-Banna's death; however, it was still a powerful force.

Various communist movements made up the Egyptian left prior to 1952. The largest and best-organized group was the Democratic Movement for National Liberation (DMNL). The communists organized labor unions, student organizations, and secret cells in the military. Communist ideas influenced a growing number of workers, impatient for jobs and better working conditions. The communists supported land reforms that would free peasants from serfdom. They also were very anti-imperialist, calling for an end to British occupation of the Suez Canal zone.[15] Although the DMNL initially supported the Free Officer's coup, Nasser saw a hidden agenda in communism and distrusted its proponents. He cracked down on communist groups in order to minimize their subversive potential and gain influence with the United States.

Between January and July 1952, some political leaders argued that Egypt needed a temporary dictator who could stabilize and reform the political order.[16] Escalating tensions with British occupation in the Suez Canal zone in late 1951 contributed to political instability. On January 26, 1952, angry crowds gathered in central Cairo to demonstrate against British occupation violence. The demonstration turned into a riot and mobs burned much of Cairo's

---

[14] Gordon, *Nasser's Blessed Movement*, 18-20.

[15] Ibid., 30-31.

[16] Ibid., 32-33.

business district. King Farouk pressed Prime Minister Nahhas to declare martial law, and then the king dismissed the government. Leaders blamed socialist groups and the Brotherhood for the violence.[17] These events prompted Nasser and his Free Officers to take action on July 23, 1952.

The Free Officer's coup took advantage of the political and social turmoil, acting as saviors from political corruption and instability. Although nominally lead by Nasser, the junta secured the appointment of a figurehead leader, General Muhammad Nagib, as prime minister and then forced King Farouk to abdicate the throne. Although Nasser rose to become a powerful figure in Egypt and the Arab region, his military coup was initially unfocused. At first, all political parties believed that the junta would impose constitutional reform, restore parliament, and then relinquish power. Many believed that Egypt had found its "just tyrant".[18] Azeema El-Husseiny and Shahenda Maklad, who participated in the 2011 uprisings, were teenage girls in 1952. They remember people expecting something to happen during that unstable time and they were happy and excited when the Free Officers took power, hoping things were changing for the better.[19]

Upon taking power, Nasser's Free Officers hoped to work with the parties and the political establishment to institute changes. Although they had a basic ideology of nationalism and social reformism that crossed political lines, the Free Officers were not ideologues. They shared these views with a younger generation that had grown disaffected with the country's political elders. The junta initially opted for an indirect role focused on purging old guard Wafd political leaders and constitutional reform. Political purges and a land redistribution policy

---

[17] Ibid., 24-25.

[18] Ibid., 37-40.

[19] Yasmine Fathi, "A tale of two Egyptian revolutions." *Ahram Online*. July 23, 2012. http://english.ahram.org.eg/NewsContent/1/139/48329/Egypt/-July-Revolution/A-tale-of-two-Egyptian-revolutions.aspx (accessed September 13, 212).

alienated the old guard, forcing Nasser to seize more control over Egyptian politics.[20] Nasser's regime did this by taking advantage of weakness and internecine struggles between and within major political forces contesting for power.

The Brotherhood and DMNL collaborated with the Free Officers, expecting to play influential roles in the new government. They urged the junta to purge corrupt political leaders and bureaucrats and restore parliamentary democracy after constitutional reform. Nasser gradually withdrew from the Brotherhood and abruptly turned on the communists. The Free Officers were committed to secularism and refused to tolerate Marxism. Nasser tried to maintain a delicate balance with the Brotherhood. He knew it was a powerful organization with strong support in the countryside, a secret paramilitary organization, and cells spread throughout the army and police.[21] The junta adopted a divide and rule policy towards it. Ultimately, the Brotherhood and the communists both suffered from factionalism and internal rivalries; therefore, they were not able to confront the rising power of Nasser's regime.

In January 1953, after political purges and a failure to unite Egypt's factionalized political parties, the junta outlawed all political parties except the Brotherhood. They then announced a three-year "transition period" of martial rule by the Command Council of the Revolution (CCR). In June of 1953, the CCR proclaimed Egypt a republic and appointed Nagib as its first president. In January 1954, after the Brotherhood resisted CCR control and internal meddling, Nasser outlawed it and arrested its leaders. The next month the CCR denounced Nagib as a tyrant and ousted him. This lead to the 1954 "March Crisis", where the CCR diffused a mass movement calling for their dismissal. Initially the junta agreed to step aside. However, this emboldened opposition leaders into revealing themselves so that state sponsored mob violence

---

[20] Gordon, *Nasser's Blessed Movement*, 12-13.

[21] Ibid., 92-99.

and coercion could silence any opposition before it could organize. Nasser then reasserted CCR control and "restored order".[22]

The "March Crisis" marked a turning point for the CCR as Nasser resolved to consolidate power and assert control over the army, press, professional associations, labor unions, and universities. In October 1954, Nasser secured a treaty providing for the evacuation of British troops from Egypt and survived an alleged assassination attempt by the Brotherhood.[23] These two events secured Nasser's domestic support, allowing him to implement his ideals of Arab nationalism, anti-imperialism, anti-Zionism, and social justice.

Nasser balanced ideology and realism to gain and consolidate power. Foreign powers played background roles that helped shape the revolutionary movement. During the 1950's the U.S. embassy's influence surpassed that of the British. The U.S. ambassador was optimistic about Nasser's government and the prospects of a long-term U.S.-Egyptian strategic relationship. Both the U.S and British played an advisory role to the CCR, fostering the Free Officer's self-confidence during a difficult formative period.[24] However, after consolidating power, Nasser confidently applied his political principles on the international stage, exploiting Cold War tensions. During the 1956 Suez Crisis, Nasser displayed bold diplomatic skill by playing the U.S., British, and Soviets against each other.

Nasser saw his coup as an inspiration to the masses to unify with his movement and form a new political order. Instead, he became very frustrated with political infighting, groups wanting to kill other groups, and Egyptians not wanting to work together for the common good.[25] He wrote that, "We needed order, but we found nothing behind us but chaos. We needed unity but we

---

[22] Ibid., 144-153.

[23] Ibid., 4.

[24] Ibid., 199-174.

[25] Gamal Abdul Nasser, *Egypt's Liberation: The Philosophy of the Revolution* (Washington D.C.: Public Affairs Press, 1955), 32-36.

found nothing behind us but dissension. We needed work, but we found behind us only indolence and sloth".[26] Nasser claimed that circumstances forced the Free Officers to leave their posts to perform a sacred duty, writing, "If the motherland had no need for us other than to stay in the ranks of the Army as professional soldiers, we would have remained there".[27] Nasser initially intended to return the government to civilian parliamentary control; however, after several attempts to establish a mass popular party, Nasser's Egypt remained under the rule of a praetorian elite. This elite was rooted in the officer corps, dominated party and state bureaucracy, and remained unwilling to open the political process.[28] The legacy of Nasser's military rule continues to be a major factor in contemporary Egyptian politics.

The Economic Environment

Throughout the early twentieth century, agriculture was Egypt's primary industry with the most arable land along the Nile River. The most important export crop was cotton, which provided necessary foreign exchange. However, the exclusive reliance on the unstable international cotton market caused economic fluctuations and inhibited the local production of foodstuffs necessary to feed a growing population. This agro-export economic model was a legacy of British colonialism.[29] Also during this period, population growth, land parcelization and gradual industrialization led to growing urbanization. From 1917 to 1947, the population went from 780,000 to 2 million in Cairo and 12.7 million to 18.8 million in the country as a whole.[30]

Rising prices, population growth, and economic stagnation marked the post World War II economic environment in Egypt. All political parties called for economic development and social

---

[26] Ibid., 34.

[27] Ibid., 38.

[28] Gordon, *Nasser's Blessed Movement*, 6-7.

[29] Alan Richards and John Waterbury, *A Political Economy of the Middle East* (Boulder, Colorado: Westview Press, 2008), 21.

[30] Botman, *Egypt from Independence to Revolution*, 21-22.

reform. At times economic issues surpassed nationalist ambitions in Egyptian politics.[31] Investing in education was one method to promote economic development. In 1950, a Wafd controlled parliament opened tuition-free secondary schools up to anyone who completed primary school. In 1957, the Egyptian parliament made tuition-free university education available to secondary school graduates and then guaranteed university graduates a government job. This misallocation of educational resources created a bloated public sector and more unemployment when limited public or private sector jobs were available for the many university graduates.[32] This economic environment fueled the turmoil and dissatisfaction that gave rise to Nasser's Free Officers.

Nasser realized the importance of developing Egypt's resources and improving economic conditions. His Aswan High Dam project was an audacious venture to do just that. The regime designed the project as a key element of Egypt's agricultural and industrial growth. Because Egypt could not fund the project, Nasser asked for and received assurance of funding from the U.S. and Britain, but they later withdrew this offer. Nasser viewed this as a Western effort to undermine Egypt's economic development, so he responded by nationalizing the Suez Canal, sparking the Suez Crisis.[33]

The Social Environment

Class conflict, Islamist fundamentalism, education, housing, health, social insurance, workers compensation, and land reform agendas dominated Egyptian social issues in the pre-Nasser era. Before the 1920s, Egypt had neither a thriving business class nor a large working class. Rural life prevailed, social mobility was limited, and family unit indoctrination reinforced submission to the authoritarian and hierarchical social structure. However, as Egypt began to

---

[31] Gordon, *Nasser's Blessed Movement*, 18-19.

[32] Richards and Waterbury, *A Political Economy of the Middle East,* 120-121.

[33] David Tal, *The 1956 War: Collusion and Rivalry in the Middle East* (Portland, OR: Frank Cass Publishers, 2001), 195-197.

industrialize and urbanize, civil society organizations such as the Muslim Brotherhood, Young Egypt, and the communist Egyptian Movement for National Liberation developed. Efforts to radicalize the working class and form labor unions bolstered both communist movements and the Brotherhood.[34]

The one issue that all Egyptians could agree on during this period was national liberation. Nasser's generation grew up under British rule, resented imperialism, and was active in nationalist politics. They felt the Pashas had ruled for their own self-gain, ignored the common man, failed to end British occupation, and had sent an ill-equipped and poorly led army to defeat in 1948. After World War II, many Egyptian officers joined secret cells organized by the Brotherhood and communist organizations. The Free Officers emerged as a secret organization as well, but they remained independent of any particular political ideology, party, or leader. Arab nationalism and social justice primarily motivated Nasser's group.[35] These became their fundamental issues after taking power.

Before the Nasser era, most Egyptian's were Muslim, but there was a small Coptic Christian minority of about eight percent. Small cosmopolitan communities of Jewish, Armenian, Greek, and Italian origin also existed. After Nasser's accession and the end of British occupation, the status of minority populations changed. Many left Egypt or took on secondary roles in business and professions.[36] This left the native Muslim Egyptians with full political and economic control.

Of all the Egyptian social movements before and during the Nasser era, the Islamist Muslim Brotherhood has been the most pervasive and enduring. Hassan Al-Banna founded the Brotherhood in 1928. He created an effective political organization that grew to an estimated half

---

[34] Botman, *Egypt from Independence to Revolution*, 6-7.

[35] Gordon, *Nasser's Blessed Movement*, 39-40.

[36] Botman, *Egypt from Independence to Revolution*, 24.

13

million members (with an even larger number of sympathizers) in less than twenty years. al-Banna primarily drew inspiration from nineteenth century Salfist ideas that explained and offered solutions for Arab decline under Western colonial powers; however, he also integrated ideals from Egyptian nationalism and socialism. He based his movement on a revival of Muslim society declaring, "Islam is the solution."[37] He saw the replacement of sharia law with man-made laws as a heretical surrender to the West. The Muslim community should embrace modernity, he preached, but avoid Westernization and secularization. al-Banna's public message called for a methodical bottom-up process for Islamizing individuals and society, after which a Muslim government based on sharia, would automatically follow. [38] However, al-Banna's message also justified violence to further the movement.

Hassan al-Banna extolled the virtues of jihad through violent combat as a way to gain honor in this life and paradise in the next. He described jihad as an obligation for spreading Islam.[39] Following this logic, some elements of the Brotherhood lost patience for the gradual approach, so al-Banna created a secret "Special Section" to train members in paramilitary skills. This group carried out attacks against British interests, participated in the 1948 war against Israel, and targeted domestic political leaders. Tensions peaked in 1948 when the government accused the Brotherhood of assassinating Prime Minister Nuqrashi. Egyptian leaders banned the organization, killed al-Banna, and incarcerated the Brotherhood's top leaders.[40]

Nasser's 1952 Free Officer coup revived the hopes of the Brotherhood. Many Free Officers had close ties to the Brotherhood, and they had fought together in Palestine. The

---

[37] Lorenzo Vidino, *The New Muslim Brotherhood in the West* (New York: Columbia University Press, 2010), 18-20, and Marc Lynch, "Islam Divided Between Salafi-jihad and the Ikhwan." *Studies in Conflict and Terrorism* 33, no. 6 (2010): 469.

[38] Vidino, *The New Muslim Brotherhood in the West*, 18-21.

[39] Hasan al-Banna, "Jihad." *Young Muslims.* Ed. Prelude Ltd. 1997. http://web.youngmuslims.ca/online_library/books/jihad/ (accessed September 6, 2012).

[40] Vidino, *The New Muslim Brotherhood in the West*, 22.

Brotherhood sought to exploit personal ties to influence the Free Officers toward an Islamic Egyptian state. Nasser initially used the Brotherhood support to strengthen his regime, but in January 1954, he banned the organization, perceiving it as a threat to his ideals of a secular state. Later that year Nasser was victim of an assassination plot, allegedly Brotherhood planned. He used the attempt as an opportunity to dismantle the organization.[41]

Nasser's repression drove a wedge between the moderate and radical wings of the Brotherhood. Imprisonment during the Nasser era fueled the extremist ideas of Brotherhood member Sayyid Qutb, whose fundamentalist ideas spread within a demoralized and angry Brotherhood. His works, such as *In the Shade of the Quran* and *Milestones*, have become classics of the greater Islamist movement. Qutb developed a doctrine that would lead many to embrace violence as a means of gaining political power, making him an ideological forefather of modern Islamist terrorism.[42] Conversely, Hassan Hubaydi rejected Qutibist ideas and led the core of the Brotherhood on a more moderate, nonviolent course. This eventually led to the reemergence of the Brotherhood as a mainstream social and political organization in the 1970s under Anwar Sadat.[43]

Nasser used the religious and social tensions in Egypt to his advantage. He not only exploited these tensions to gain and consolidate power, but he also used them diplomatically. He harnessed Egyptian anger over the creation of an Israeli state, the legacy of European colonialism, and poor social conditions to build a powerful regime.

---

[41] Ibid., 23.

[42] Lynch, "Islam Divided Between Salafi-jihad and the Ikhwan.", 469-470, and Vidino, *The New Muslim Brotherhood in the West*, 24-25.

[43] Ibid.

The Military Environment

Egyptian military capability improved during the Nasser era; however, it would never match the performance of Western armed forces. Under British occupation, the Egyptian military was primarily a defensive constabulary force. It was not until the 1936 Anglo-Egyptian treaty that Britain granted Egypt partial sovereignty over its military forces. Egyptian forces still relied on the British for training and equipment.[44] After World War II, Egypt gained full sovereignty from Britain. In 1948, Egypt joined with other Arab countries in opposing the founding of Israel.[45] Defeat at the hands of the Israelis was a defining event for the Egyptian Army. Trapped in the Fallujah pocket, Nasser and his comrades were especially bitter. This crucible united them against the king and his generals for sending them to war with inferior equipment and poor leadership.[46] This resentment solidified in Nasser's Free Officer movement and the 1952 coup.

Nasser and the Free Officers purged many colonels and all but two general officers from the armed forces. Nasser promoted his close friend from the Fallujah pocket, Abdel Hakim Amer, to commander in chief of the armed forces. With Nasser's support, Amer began stressing professionalization of the officer corps; however, political loyalty remained an important consideration for promotion. Eventually political connections overrode professional concerns. This was exemplified by the poor leadership and political subterfuge of Field Marshal Amer during 1956 Suez Crisis and 1967 Six-Day War.[47]

Nasser's arms deal with Czechoslovakia in 1955 allowed Egypt access to sophisticated Eastern Bloc military hardware. However, this was of little advantage to Egyptian forces due to their limited ability to integrate complex weapon systems. Rigid class separation divided the

---

[44] Gordon, *Nasser's Blessed Movement*, 41-45.

[45] Kenneth M. Pollack, *Arabs at War: Military Effectiveness, 1948-1991* (Lincoln: University of Nebraska Press, 2002), 15.

[46] Nasser, *Egypt's Liberation*, 94-98.

[47] Pollack, *Arabs at War*, 86-89.

officers from enlisted personnel. This caused mistrust and contempt, which weakened cohesion and discipline. It also made complex offensive operations requiring initiative impossible for Egyptian forces. Egypt could fight fixed defensive battles, but counterattacks or other mobile operations rarely succeeded.[48] Recognizing these weaknesses, Egyptian leaders emphasized positional warfare and fixed defenses. This made them vulnerable to maneuver warfare. Nasser could not depend on military means to prevail in international conflicts. Instead, he relied on diplomacy.

The 1956 Suez Crisis

The British occupied Egypt from 1882 to 1956. This allowed them to maintain control of the Suez Canal, but it also produced anti-British societies and riots. The 1956 Suez Crisis was the climax of Egypt's decades-long struggle to cast off British domination. World War II significantly weakened the British Empire. Its economic recovery depended on affordable petroleum shipped through the Suez Canal. By the 1950s, two-thirds of Britain's oil supply traveled through the Suez Canal. It was impossible for Britain to meet domestic demand by shipping around Africa. However, the British had difficulty maintaining control of Egypt, so they turned to rising U.S. influence to fill the power vacuum.[49]

In 1955, Nasser signed a treaty ending British military occupation of the Canal Zone. At the same time, he threatened British influence in Iraq and Jordan by opposing the Baghdad pact and supporting pan-Arab nationalism. Additionally, Nasser threatened French influence in North Africa, by supporting the Algerian insurgency. Cross-border partisan raids on Israeli settlements from Gaza, Egypt, Jordan, and Syria threatened Israel. The Israelis retaliated by raiding Gaza. In response, Nasser blocked the Tiran straights denying Israel access to the Red Sea and concluded

---

[48] Derek Varble, *The Suez Crisis 1956* (Oxford: Osprey Publishing Limited, 2003), 19-20.
[49] Ibid., 11-12.

an arms deal with Soviet Czechoslovakia. David Ben-Gurion saw these actions as an existential threat to Israel. The events leading up to the 1956 Crisis caused Israel, France, Britain, and the U.S. to favor Arab fragmentation and Nasser became their main threat.[50]

The Eisenhower administration tried to nurture a supportive relationship with revolutionary Egypt; however, Nasser's turn to Soviet military support angered Washington. American and British leaders developed a plan for covert regime change in Egypt. As part of this plan, they withdrew funding for the Aswan High Dam project on July 19, 1956. Nasser responded by nationalizing the Suez Canal on July 26. This ended the Paris-based Suez Canal Company's concession for Canal control and outraged Britain and France.[51] They decided to overthrow Nasser, leading to the Suez War in October.

U.S. leaders favored Nasser's removal, but they did not believe the liabilities of military action outweighed the benefits. They pressured Britain and France to avoid military confrontation and give covert and diplomatic efforts more time. Britain and France decided to pursue a military option anyway. They secretly brought Israel in on the plan and left the U.S. on the sidelines. Their assumption that world and domestic opinion would support retaking the Canal by force proved to be false.[52] After ten days of fighting to gain control of the Suez Canal and the Sinai, intense international pressure forced Britain, France, and Israel to withdraw to pre-conflict borders.

Nasser emerged from the Suez War a hero both in Egypt and in the Arab world, despite a mediocre performance by the Egyptian military. Arabs saw Nasser as the conqueror of European colonialism and Zionism because Britain, France, and Israel left the Sinai and Northern Canal

---

[50] Pollack, *Arabs at War,* 30. and Varble, *The Suez Crisis 1956,* 13-14.

[51] Varble, *The Suez Crisis 1956,* 14.

[52] Ibid., 21-27.

Zone.[53] In 1958, Nasser capitalized on his pan-Arab influence by linking Egypt and Syria in a United Arab Republic. Pro-Nasser factions emerged in places like Iraq. Nasser's stature as a pan-Arab leader lasted until his defeat in the 1967 Six-Day War.[54] Nasser's pan-Arab movement dwindled throughout the late twentieth century.

The Current Revolutionary Environment in Egypt

The event now known as the "Arab Awakening" has brought new opportunities and challenges for the MENA region. On Dec. 17, 2010, in a final act of hopelessness, Mohammed Bouazizi set himself ablaze in front of a government building in Tunisia. This sparked civil unrest that toppled autocratic regimes in Tunisia, Libya, and Egypt and opened the door to democratic political development.[55] *Washington Post* columnist David Ignatius saw it as a "global political awakening", a demand for democracy and justice. He cites Brent Scowcroft who described it as a "yearning for dignity".[56] These outward symbols are valid, but they fail to identify the underlying conditions that drove Egyptians to revolt against the Mubarak regime.

Since the 1950s, Egypt has experienced some of the highest population growth in the world. This combined with rising food costs, high unemployment, and stagnant economic growth shaped Egypt's current revolutionary environment. These conditions will not go away with the old regime. Although there is a liberal democratic constituency in Egypt, Islamist movements led by the Muslim Brotherhood have dominated Egypt's recent elections. The ruling military council attempted a democratic transition to civilian control; however, it has resisted relinquishing control

---

[53] Pollack, *Arabs at War*, 47-48.

[54] Varble, *The Suez Crisis 1956,* 84.

[55] Ellen Knickmeyer, "The Arab World's Youth Army" In *Revolution in the Arab World: Tunisia, Egypt, and the Unmaking of an Era,* by Foreign Policy, by Foreign Policy, ed. Marc Lynch, B Glasser Susan and Blake Hounshell (n.p.: The Slate Group, A Division of The Washington Post Company, 2011), 122-123.

[56] David Ignatius, "What Happens When the Arab Spring Turns to Summer?" *Foreign Policy.* April 22, 2011. http://www.foreignpolicy.com/articles/2011/04/22/what_happens_when_the_arab_spring_turns_to_summer (accessed September 28, 2011).

of its economic benefits and foreign policy decisions to a Brotherhood-led government. The stakes of Egypt's revolutionary gamble are high. The future stability of the Middle East and the global order depends on the steadiness of Egypt's new government, and its ability to solve social and economic ills.

The Political Environment

Little is certain in current Egyptian politics. On June 30, 2012, the Supreme Council of the Armed Force's (SCAF) Field Marshal Mohamed Tantawi handed over power to the Brotherhood's Mohamed Morsi. Stating that SCAF was fulfilling its promises to relinquish power, Tantawi added, "We now have an elected president, who assumed Egypt's rule through a free and direct vote reflecting the will of Egyptians."[57] However, on 17 June, only days before the presidential election run-off, SCAF dissolved the Brotherhood-dominated parliament and decreed new constitutional limitations on presidential power.[58] Morsi sought ways to challenge SCAF's unwillingness to transition full executive and legislative power by reviewing legal options to reinstate the elected parliament. Meanwhile, demonstrators gathered in front of the presidential palace on 21 June demanding the release of political prisoners, better pay, and more jobs from Morsi's government.[59] After eighteen months of revolutionary transition, Egypt had a president again; however, the reformation of its government and economy was just beginning.

---

[57] Mary Casey and Jennifer Parker, "New Egyptian president looks to reinstate parliament." *Foreign Policy.* July 2, 2012.
http://mideast.foreignpolicy.com/posts/2012/07/02/new_egyptian_president_looks_to_reinstate_parliament (accessed July 6, 2012).

[58] Kareem Fahim and Dina Salah Amer, "Uncertainties Underlie the Celebrations in Cairo." *The New York Times.* June 18, 2012. http://www.nytimes.com/2012/06/19/world/middleeast/uncertainty-underlies-celebrations-in-cairo.html?_r=1&ref=world (accessed July 7, 2012).

[59] Reuters, "Egypt's new president faces burden of expectation." *Ahram Online.* July 2, 2012. http://english.ahram.org.eg/NewsContent/1/64/46684/Egypt/Politics-/Egypts-new-president-faces-burden-of-expectation.aspx (accessed July 7, 2012).

Worries about a post-Mubarak government started well before February 2011. In September of 2010, foreign policy scholars and former U.S. Government officials warned the Obama administration to prepare for an unstable power transition in Egypt.[60] Before the revolution, Gregory Aftandilian developed seven possible presidential succession scenarios in a study for the U.S. Army War College. Aftandilian's scenarios identify many of the key political figures and interests that have unfolded over the last two years.[61] One of these figures, Muhammad El-Baradei, returned to Egypt in late 2009 as a national hero and began calling for democratic reforms. He formed the National Association for Change to assemble opposition against the regime. This organization rallied the support of young intellectuals from the April 6 Youth (A6Y) movement and members of the Brotherhood. In December 2010, El-Baradei mustered nearly 1 million signatures on a petition demanding democratic changes.[62] The political environment in Egypt was ripe for revolution in January 2011.

Socially active Egyptian youth groups, such as A6Y, organized the massive protest of January 25, 2011 to demonstrate against police brutality, corruption, and poor economic conditions. They primarily used online media and cell phones to manage their protests, since the regime could not suppress the internet without completely shutting it down. They had studied non-violent protest methods that would be difficult for the regime to counter.[63] Revolutionary sentiment was high due to the peaceful overthrow of Tunisia's dictator the month before. Exceeding expectations, the activist leaders drew in tens of thousands of protesters to Tahrir

---

[60] Rozen, Laura. "Former officials, scholars warned of coming instability in Egypt." *Politico.* January 30, 2011. http://www.politico.com/blogs/laurarozen/0111/They_told_us_Former_officials_scholars_warned_of_coming_instability_in_Egypt html (accessed July 14, 2012).

[61] Gregory Aftandilian, *Presidential Succession Scenarios in Egypt and Their Impact on U.S.-Egyptian Strategic Relations.* Monograph, Carlisle, PA: Strategic Studies Institute, United States Army War College, September 2011.

[62] Aftandilian, *Presidential Succession Scenarios in Egypt*, 25. The April 6 Youth movement and its involvement with Muhammad El-Baradei is discussed further in the social environment section.

[63] Michael Kirk, "Revolution in Cairo" *Frontline,* DVD (Boston: PBS Distribution, 2011).

Square on 25 January.[64] Capitalizing on success, the activists planned for a larger demonstration

on Friday, the 28th, but on that day Mubarak shut down internet and cell phone services to try to

quell the protests. Instead, this provided more fuel to the anti-Mubarak movement and drove more

protesters to Tahrir Square.[65] This "Day of Rage" transformed the demonstrations into a massive

revolutionary movement.

Initially the activists made limited demands for police and economic reforms. On the

"Day of Rage" protestors fought with Mubarak's security police. Demonstrators burned down

police headquarters, and the government called in the Army to restore order. The protesters'

demands escalated, eventually calling for an immediate end to Mubarak's rule. In the days that

followed, the regime tried to suppress the revolution. Pro-Mubarak supporters fought with

demonstrators in Tahrir Square on 2-3 February.[66] The police arrested many A6Y leaders and El-

Baradei followers.[67] The regime also coordinated an anti-foreigner campaign to intimidate and

silence journalists reporting on the protests. Government efforts to crush the protests only

hardened the activists' resolve.[68] The Egyptian Army refused to use lethal force and tried to

remain neutral. This gave the protesters hope and protection from police and regime supporters.

Although Mubarak tried to make limited concessions and promised not to run for reelection in the

fall, the people of Egypt had discovered their power and called for his immediate removal.[69]

---

[64] Ibid.

[65] David Wolman, "The Instigators" *The Atavist.* no. 4 (Brooklyn, New York: Atavist Inc., April/May 2011), 8.

[66] Mohammad Bamyeh, "The Egyptian Revolution: First Impressions from the Field." *Middle East Institute.* February 8, 2011. http://www.mei.nus.edu.sg/blog/country/egypt/the-egyptian-revolution-first-impressions-from-the-field (accessed September 4, 2012).

[67] Wolman, "The Instigators", 8.

[68] Peter Bouckaert, "February 9: Egypt's Foreigner Blame Game" In *Revolution in the Arab World: Tunisia, Egypt, and the Unmaking of an Era*, by Foreign Policy, ed. Marc Lynch, B Glasser Susan and Blake Hounshell (n.p.: The Slate Group, A Division of The Washington Post Company, 2011), 103.

[69] Kirk, "Revolution in Cairo"

The demonstrations drew in popular support across generational, political, and religious lines. Eyewitness Cairo journalist, Ashraf Khalil, describes seeing young and old, male and female, and Christian and Muslim people in the crowds. A woman in her mid-50s came out with her two teenage sons showing them that it is possible to demonstrate peacefully for change. Khalil also reported that the Muslim Brotherhood did not directly participate in the early protests.[70] Used to political repression, older leaders of the Brotherhood initially wanted to keep their distance from the secular protests. However, Brotherhood youth leaders joined in to support the movement. Their ability to organize and provide social services allowed the crowds of protesters to remain in Tahrir Square for over two weeks. Realizing the secular nature of the demonstrations and wanting to promote unity, the Brotherhood discouraged its followers from using religious symbols and rhetoric.[71] The Brotherhood proclaimed solidarity with the civil protests by demanding democracy, economic reforms, and social justice. When pro-regime thugs attacked the demonstrators, Brotherhood members were in the front lines trying to push them back.[72] Although young secular activists ignited and lead the revolution, the well-organized Brotherhood capitalized on it.

On the night of 10 February, Mubarak addressed the country and many expected him to resign. Instead, he continued to discuss reforms without immediately relinquishing power. Angry crowds in Tahrir Square discussed taking violent action. They demanded that the Army choose a side.[73] El-Baredei tweeted, "Egypt will explode. Army must save the country now."[74] The next

---

[70] Ashraf Khalil, "January 25: Tear Gas on the Day of Rage" In *Revolution in the Arab World: Tunisia, Egypt, and the Unmaking of an Era,* by Foreign Policy, ed. Marc Lynch, B Glasser Susan and Blake Hounshell (n.p.: The Slate Group, A Division of the Washington Post Company, 2011), 74-75.

[71] Martin Smith and Charles M. Sennott. "The Brothers" *Frontline,* DVD (Boston: PBS Distribution, 2011).

[72] Ibid.

[73] Ibid.

23

evening, newly-appointed Vice President Omar Suleiman announced that Mubarak had resigned and relinquished power to a transitional military government.[75]

Opposition leaders called for a new government of national unity, the dissolution of the state security apparatus, an overhaul of the police, the complete independence of the press, and free and fair elections.[76] SCAF announced it would oversee new parliamentary and presidential elections and a constitutional revision process to transfer power to a free, democratic civilian authority.[77] On 19 March, a referendum approved temporary amendments to the constitution allowing parliamentary elections in June of 2011 with presidential elections to follow. Full constitutional revision would wait until after parliamentary elections. SCAF later postponed parliamentary elections until November 2011 to give new political parties more time to organize and campaign.[78] This opened the door for Egypt's diverse political factions to organize parties and contest for power.

Egypt's transition to democratic government was fraught with difficulty. Middle East expert Fawaz Gerges explained the transition period as a fierce power struggle along ideological, religious, and social lines with the military trying to maintain its privileges.[79] Three primary groups with differing interests battled for power in the new government. The first of these, SCAF,

---

[74] Ashraf Khalil, "February 10: We Need to Drag Him From His Palace" In *Revolution in the Arab World: Tunisia, Egypt, and the Unmaking of an Era*, by Foreign Policy, ed. Marc Lynch, B Glasser Susan and Blake Hounshell (n.p.: The Slate Group, A Division of The Washington Post Company, 2011), 109.

[75] Wolman, "The Instigators", 9.

[76] Blake Hounshell, "February 11: Pharaoh is Dead, Long Live Pharaoh?" In *Revolution in the Arab World: Tunisia, Egypt, and the Unmaking of an Era*, by Foreign Policy, ed. Marc Lynch, B Glasser Susan and Blake Hounshell (n.p.: The Slate Group, A Division of The Washington Post Company, 2011), 114.

[77] Ashraf Khalil, "February 12: After the Party" In *Revolution in the Arab World: Tunisia, Egypt, and the Unmaking of an Era*, by Foreign Policy, ed. Marc Lynch, B Glasser Susan and Blake Hounshell (n.p.: The Slate Group, A Division of The Washington Post Company, 2011), 117.

[78] Jeremy M. Sharp, *Egypt in Transition,* Report for Congress (Washington D.C.: Congressional Research Service, August 23, 2011), 8-9.

[79] Edmund Blair and Marwa Awad. "Egypt's army faces wrath for delaying civilian rule" *Al Arabiya News.* November 22, 2011. http://english.alarabiya net/articles/2011/11/22/178548 html (accessed September 2, 2012).

attempted to manage its exit from government while retaining its economic benefits and influence over foreign policy. Michigan State professor Mohammed Ayoob argued that the military choreographed Mubarak's removal to distance itself from the doomed president and demonstrate that the military was not opposed to the protesters' demands and aspirations. However, he emphasizes that Egypt's officer corps would not relinquish its corporate interests for the sake of popular welfare.[80] Egypt's military leaders were also hesitant to disrupt the flow of $1.5 billion per year in U.S. economic and military assistance, and they pledged their adherence to the 1979 treaty with Israel.[81] SCAF also sought to appease the Brotherhood, since it was most likely to control the next government.[82]

The Islamist movements were the second contending group. They included the more moderate Muslim Brotherhood and the more conservative Salafist groups. The Brotherhood, the stronger of the two, made an effort to distance itself from Salafist ideology and appear moderate. The Brotherhood reached out to secular and liberal groups by forming alliances with major parties and working closely with SCAF.[83] In June 2011, the Brotherhood's Freedom and Justice Party (FJP) formed a coalition with the secular Wafd party, Egypt's oldest liberal political party.

---

[80] Mohammed Ayoob, "The Tyrant is Dead, But What About His Tyranny?" In *Revolution in the Arab World: Tunisia, Egypt, and the Unmaking of an Era*, by Foreign Policy, ed. Marc Lynch, B Glasser Susan and Blake Hounshell (n.p.: The Slate Group, A Division of The Washington Post Company, 2011), 211.

[81] Sharp, *Egypt in Transition,* 8, 12-13.

[82] Eric Trager, "Egypt's Triangular Power Struggle" *The Washington Institute,* July 22, 2011. http://www.washingtoninstitute.org/policy-analysis/view/egypts-triangular-power-struggle (accessed September 6, 2012).

[83] Trager, "Egypt's Triangular Power Struggle". Trager estimates the MB at 750,000 members. Since Mubarak's fall, it has opened thirteen new local headquarters throughout the country, inaugurated headquarters for its FJP in most governorates, and cemented an alliance with twenty-seven other parties, many of which sacrificed their demands for delayed elections in exchange for the MB's cooperation in drafting electoral procedures.

Both parties tried to expand their base to win a majority in parliamentary elections.[84] However, this coalition only lasted until August 2011.

The Brotherhood used a gradualist approach to achieve its goals. Eric Trager of the Washington Institute argues that democratic elections provided a peaceful way for the well-organized Brotherhood to gain power and create an Islamic state.

> For its part, the Brotherhood is widely expected to win a plurality in the elections because of its significant mobilization capabilities…The Brotherhood's primary aim is to hold elections as soon as possible, before other parties can organize effectively enough to become competitive. It would then use its electoral success to control the subsequent constitutional drafting process, through which it hopes to establish an Islamic state.[85]

The Brotherhood maintained a delicate balance between supporting SCAF's efforts to expedite the election process and demonstrating unity with the protestors.

The final coalition fighting for influence in Egypt's post revolution environment was pro-democracy protesters supported by liberal-secular parties. Maintaining the demands of the January revolution, these groups wanted to prosecute and imprison former regime officials, end military detentions and trials, cancel emergency laws, reform the Ministry of Interior, and establish a democratic political order. Although they maintained significant mobilizing capabilities and continued mass demonstrations, they were unable to translate that into a cohesive political organization. Initially, the protesters demanded a longer transition period so that they could organize effective political parties and draft a new constitution before holding elections. They dropped these demands to ensure continued Brotherhood support of their demonstrations.[86] El-Baredei initially tried to lead and organize this group, but he dropped out of the presidential race in January 2012, protesting that SCAF control and Brotherhood domination skewed the

---

[84] Leila Fadel, "Egypt's Muslim Brotherhood forms coalition with liberal party" *The Washington Post*, June 13, 2011. http://www.washingtonpost.com/world/egypts-muslim-brotherhood-forms-coalition-with-liberal-party/2011/06/13/AGQI7OTH_story.html (accessed September 6, 2012).

[85] Trager, "Egypt's Triangular Power Struggle".

[86] Ibid.

process against secular democracy. Realizing that liberal democratic change was not happening in the short term, El-Baredei began looking longer term to reunify the protest movement under the new Dustour Party in April 2012.[87] The tensions between SCAF, Islamist, and secular interests shaped the contest for power during Egypt's transition process, and the Brotherhood prevailed.

These tensions were on display during July 2011. On 8 July, secular and leftist groups began a month long protest in Tahrir Square to demand "supra-constitutional" principles that would guarantee a secular democratic constitution. This stirred up tensions with Islamists who were demanding sharia law as the basis for the next constitution. Activists brokered an agreement with Islamists to focus on the unity of the revolution rather than divisive demands. However, on 29 July, Salafists and other religious parties took over the protests, turning a day of unity in Tahrir Square into a highly polarized call for the imposition of sharia law. The Brotherhood initially joined in with the Salifists; however, they were split between maintaining unity with secular groups and supporting calls for sharia. Two days later, secular protesters left Tahrir Square after alienating SCAF and most Egyptians.[88] The month long protests diminished the legitimacy of secular democracy activists, giving Islamists control over the revolutionary movement.

These tensions continued during the lead up to parliamentary elections. When it appeared that Islamist parties would dominate the new government, SCAF tried to delay presidential elections until late 2012 or early 2013. The Brotherhood led new demonstrations demanding presidential elections in April, immediately after parliamentary elections. Trying to restore order, the military clashed with protesters, causing the loss of lives. The Brotherhood then pulled back,

---

[87] Reuters, "Newly formed political party will get Egyptian revolution back on track and one day rule the country, says its founder reform leader Mohamed ElBaredei" *ITN Source,* April 28, 2012. http://www.itnsource.com/shotlist/RTV/2012/04/28/RTV1304912/ (accessed September 6, 2012).

[88] Marc Lynch, "Tahrir turning points." In *Islamists in a Changing Middle East*, by Foreign Policy, ed. Marc Lynch (n.p.: The FP Group, a division of the Washington Post Company, 2012), 70-72.

urging caution.[89] These clashes caused protesters to lose trust in the army and SCAF leaders. Activists equated Field Marshal Tantawi to Mubarak, since he was holding on to power and suppressing the revolution.[90] State violence under its oversight gradually turned the Egyptian populace against SCAF. Eventually SCAF allowed elections to proceed as planned which benefited the better-organized Islamist groups. The liberal-secular parties did not have time to make an effective showing in the elections.

During the parliamentary elections, the Brotherhood's FJP and the Salafist al-Nour Party received over two-thirds of the seats.[91] SCAF leaders prepared to celebrate the first anniversary of the revolution and successful parliamentary elections. However, youth groups such as A6Y refused to celebrate until Egypt's leaders met their demands for social justice, freedom of expression, corruption reforms, and dignity.[92]

Drafting a new constitution became a priority for the new parliament. Early in 2012, the new parliament selected a 100 member constitutional assembly. However, Islamists dominated the assembly. Liberals and Coptic Christians pulled out of the assembly in protest. Parliament replaced them with more Islamists. In April, an Egyptian court suspended parliament's

---

[89] The New York Times, "Muslim Brotherhood (Egypt)" *The New York Times,* Sept 7, 2012. http://topics nytimes.com/top/reference/timestopics/organizations/m/muslim_brotherhood_egypt/index.htm l (accessed September 9, 2012).

[90] Blair and Awad. "Egypt's army faces wrath for delaying civilian rule".

[91] AFP, "Muslim Brotherhood wins nearly half the seats in the Egyptian parliament" *Al Arabiya News,* January 21, 2012. http://english.alarabiya.net/articles/2012/01/21/189694 html (accessed September 2, 2012) and Al Arabiya with Agencies, "Islamist party wins majority seats in upper house of Egypt's parliament" *Al Arabia News,* February 25, 2012. http://english.alarabiya net/articles/2012/02/25/196984.html (accessed September 2, 2012).

In the lower house, the FJP won 47 percent, Salafist al-Nour gained 24 percent and the liberal secularist Wafd Party gained 9 percent. In the upper house FJP gained 59 percent of the seats, al-Nour gained 26 percent and the Wafd Party gained 8 percent.

[92] AFP, "Muslim Brotherhood wins nearly half the seats in the Egyptian parliament".

constitutional assembly, claiming it was illegitimate.[93] Since SCAF dissolved parliament in June

2012, the process of drafting a new Egyptian constitution was still in process after Morsi assumed

power.

Before the parliamentary elections, the Brotherhood pledged not to run a presidential

candidate, alleviating fears of an Islamist takeover. However, in March 2012 the FJP nominated

Khariat el-Shater, a chief strategist and financer for the Brotherhood. Shater was a political

prisoner under Mubarak. His candidacy outraged liberals who wondered what other pledges of

moderation the Brotherhood would abandon.[94] Former leading member of the Brotherhood,

Kamal al-Helbawi, saw Shater's candidacy as the result of a secret agreement between SCAF and

the Brotherhood. He alludes to a "quid pro quo" agreement where SCAF supported a

Brotherhood candidate so that the Brotherhood would not challenge the military's economic and

political privileges.[95] No matter what deals where made behind the scenes, the balance of power

upheld candidates who were favorable to SCAF and the Brotherhood.

In April, the High Election Commission disqualified Shater due to his conviction on

political charges. The FJP had Mohamed Morsi ready to take his place. Morsi spent the ten years

before 2011 as a spokesman for the Brotherhood's political wing. In 2007 when the Brotherhood

first considered forming a political party, Morsi oversaw the drafting of a political platform

stating that the Brotherhood wanted both a tolerant constitutional democracy and an Islamic

---

[93] Al Arabiya with Agencies, "Egyptian court suspends Islamists-dominated constitutional assembly" *Al Arabiya News,* April 10, 2012. http://english.alarabiya.net/articles/2012/04/10/206737 html (accessed September 16, 2012).

[94] The New York Times, "Muslim Brotherhood (Egypt)".

[95] Amira Fouda, "Muslim Brotherhood conspired with military council to field presidential candidate: former member" *Al Arabiya News,* April 02, 2012. http://english.alarabiya net/articles/2012/04/02/204903.html (accessed September 16, 2012) and Marc.Lynch, "The Muslim Brotherhood's Presidential Gambit" In *Islamists in a Changing Middle East*, by Foreign Policy, ed. Marc Lynch (n.p.: The FP Group, a division of the Washington Post Company, 2012), 91-92. The Brotherhood presidential nomination surprised Middle East professor Marc Lynch who has interviewed many Brotherhood senior leaders, including Shater, over the years. Lynch also acknowledges the possibility of collusion between the Brotherhood and SCAF.

state.[96] While campaigning, Morsi's message highlighted his support of the revolutionary movement and its accomplishment of ending Mubarak's rule. He tried to reassure voters that the FJP would not force religious ideals on them. "God gave people the right to believe what they wish and to practice what they want," he said. "We have no right to force our ideas on them." However, he also highlighted that he would not bow to American or Israeli interests.[97] Leading up to the first round of presidential elections in May, Morsi and the other four major candidates, Ahmed Shafiq, Hamdeen Sabbahi, Abdel-Moneim Abul-Futouh, and Amr Moussa made their case to Egyptian voters.[98]

The first round of the presidential election was in May 2012. With 44 percent voter turnout, Morsi received over 25 percent of the vote, Shafiq 24 percent, Sabbahi 22 percent, Abul-Fotouh 18 percent, and Moussa ended up with 11 percent. This meant that Morsi and Shafiq would face each other in the runoff election in June 2012.[99] After the runoff election, the High Election Commission declared Morsi the new Egyptian President. According to election officials,

---

[96] The New York Times, "Muslim Brotherhood (Egypt)". Mohamed Morsi has a PhD in engineering from the University of Southern California.

[97] Yasmine Fathi, "Brotherhood's Morsi promises national 'renaissance' at Alex campaign rally" *Ahram Online.* April 25, 2012. http://english.ahram.org.eg/NewsContent/36/122/40127/Brotherhoods-Morsi-promises-national-renaissance-a.aspx (accessed September 16, 2012).

[98] Ekram Ibrahim, Zeinab El Gundi, Yasmine Fathi, and Hatem Maher, *Ahram Online Presidential Elections 2012,* April 2, 2012. http://english.ahram.org.eg/UI/Front/Pelections2012.aspx (accessed September 16, 2012). Shafiq was a former commander of the Egyptian Air Force and civil aviation minister. Mubarak appointed him prime minister four days into the revolution. Although Shafiq tried to appeal to the liberal minded protest movement, his ties to the Mubarak era reduced his popularity. Sabbahi was a long time opposition leader who supported the revolutionary activists. He was an outspoken critic of the U.S. and Israel. One of his campaign promises was to put the issue of maintaining the Camp David peace agreement before a popular referendum. Abul-Futouh was a politically active member of the Muslim Brotherhood before and after the revolution, however his views represented the more liberal wing of the Brotherhood. When he announced his candidacy for president in May 2011, the more conservative members of the Brotherhood dismissed Abul-Futouh claiming he had broken party rules by running for president. Moussa had served as foreign minister under Mubarak and as secretary-general of the Arab League. He had liberal views on social issues and supported the revolutionary activists. A staunch critic of Israel, Moussa called for revisiting the Camp David treaty.

[99] Ahram Online, "Relive vote count in 1st round of Egypt presidential race: How Morsi and Shafiq moved on" *Ahram Online,* May 25, 2012. http://english.ahram.org.eg/NewsContent/36/122/42755/Relive-vote-count-in-st-round-of-Egypt-presidentia.aspx (accessed September 16, 2012).

Morsi won 52 percent of the vote.[100] Because of his close ties to Mubarak, some Egyptians claimed there would be a war in the streets between protesters and security forces if Shafik took power. Since the runoff was between Morsi and Shafik, liberal-secularists felt they did not have a good choice.[101] Only about 51 percent of eligible voters turned out for the runoff election.[102] Their choice was to either empower the Brotherhood or go back to a holdover from the Mubarak era.

The Brotherhood's FJP gained the most from recent elections. It is the most organized non-military political group in Egypt. There is some diversity of political opinion within the Brotherhood. The younger generation believes in democracy and pluralism, but the old guard is still committed to a sharia state.[103] The Salafist coalition, al-Nour, was the second largest winner in Egypt's elections. Linked to Wahabist groups in Saudi Arabia, it represents the most fundamentalist Islamist groups. Salafist ideas provided inspiration to Al-Qaeda and similar terrorist movements.[104] Shater, described as the Brotherhood's chief policy architect, argues that the Islamist electoral victories represent an indisputable democratic mandate for an Islamic government.[105]

There is a significant debate both within and outside Egypt over the true intentions of the Brotherhood. Journalist, Robert Kaplan compares the recent Egyptian revolution to the 1978-79 Iranian revolution. He points out that Shia Islamists hijacked the Iranian revolution, although it

---

[100] The New York Times, "Muslim Brotherhood (Egypt)".

[101] Tom Perry, "Egypt's Muslim Brotherhood must face up to historic duty" *Al Arabia New,* May 31, 2012. http://english.alarabiya net/articles/2012/05/31/217808 html (accessed September 16, 2012).

[102] W. Andrew Terrill, "Breaking News Analysis: The Future of the U.S. Political and Military Relationship with Egypt" *Strategic Studies Institute, U.S. Army War College,* July 9, 2012. http://www.strategicstudiesinstitute.army.mil/index.cfm/articles/Future-of-the-US-Political-and-Military-Relationship-with-Egypt/2012/07/09 (accessed September 6, 2012).

[103] Smith and Sennott. "The Brothers".

[104] Lynch, "Islam Divided Between Salafi-jihad and the Ikhwan.", 469-470.

[105] The New York Times, "Muslim Brotherhood (Egypt)".

began over issues such as unemployment, tyranny, and social justice. Kaplan argues that the Brotherhood is a moderate Sunni Islamist movement and is not likely to hijack democracy in Egypt.[106] Likewise, Middle East scholar Marc Lynch, argues that the Brotherhood leaders speak the language of democracy and peaceful political participation and reject the extremist methods of Al Qaeda and other terrorist groups. However, Lynch also argues that the Brotherhood is committed to spreading a conservative Islamic society and is hostile to Israel and to U.S. foreign policy.[107] No matter what its underlying goals are, the Brotherhood limited religious symbols and rhetoric during the revolution to portray a moderate stance, especially in front of foreign media.[108] However, this could also be evidence of the Brotherhood's pragmatic gradual approach for achieving its long-term goal of an Islamic caliphate based on sharia law.

The Brotherhood professes commitment to democracy, inclusiveness, and civil liberties; however, it also professes commitment to its founding objectives. Spokesmen for the Brotherhood have insisted that Egypt is a Muslim country and should implement sharia law, although there is much debate on what their version of a sharia state would look like.[109] *The Jerusalem Post* reported on a Brotherhood election rally in May 2012. At the rally, an Islamist cleric rallied support for Morsi by calling for a caliphate with a capital in Jerusalem. When Morsi spoke to the crowd, he seemed to agree with the cleric saying, "Yes, Jerusalem is our goal. We shall pray in Jerusalem, or die as martyrs on its threshold."[110] This may just be campaign rhetoric with Morsi playing to his loyal supporters. However, the article also quotes Raymond Stock, an

---

[106] Robert D. Kaplan, "The New Arab World Order" In *Revolution in the Arab World: Tunisia, Egypt, and the Unmaking of an Era*, by Foreign Policy, ed. Marc Lynch, B Glasser Susan and Blake Hounshell (n.p.: The Slate Group, A Division of The Washington Post Company, 2011), 173.

[107] Lynch, "Islam Divided Between Salafi-jihad and the Ikhwan.", 467-498.

[108] Smith and Sennott. "The Brothers".

[109] Al Arabiya with Agencies, "Egyptians wrap up 2nd round of phased election; Islamists set to dominate" *Al Arabiya,* December 15, 2011. http://english.alarabiya net/articles/2011/12/15/182796 html (accessed September 6, 2012).

[110] Oren Kessler, "Egypt Islamist vows global caliphate in Jerusalem" *The Jerusalem Post,* May 08, 2012. http://www.jpost.com/MiddleEast/Article.aspx?ID=269074&R=R1 (accessed May 15, 2012).

American translator and academic who has spent several years in Egypt. He said, "This is what the Muslim Brotherhood really stands for: the extermination of Israel – and Jews everywhere – as well as the spread and control of radical Islam over the world."[111] If Stock is right then Morsi's FJP will retreat from U.S. alignment and renew hostility towards Israel.

The Egyptian parliament's stance toward Israel is another indicator of Egypt's anti-Zionist views. In March 2012, after Israeli warplanes attacked the Gaza strip, Egypt's parliament unanimously approved a resolution calling for "the expulsion from Egypt of the Israeli ambassador and the recall of Egypt's envoy from Tel Aviv". It also called for a halt to gas exports to Israel. The text continued, "Egypt will never be the friend, partner or ally of the Zionist entity which we consider as the first enemy of Egypt and the Arab nation".[112] Although SCAF refused to implement this resolution, a popularly-elected Egyptian government is likely to continue the anti-Israel message.

Currently there is a power struggle between Morsi's Brotherhood and military leadership that will determine the future direction of Egypt. Middle East scholar Nathan Toronto argues that the true test of revolutionary change will come if the new government challenges the oligarchic hold current and former military officers have on Egypt's economy.[113] At this point, indicators show Morsi and the Brotherhood gaining an advantage. In August 2012, Morsi canceled the constitutional amendments SCAF had instituted shortly before he was elected president and appointed senior judge Mahamoud Mekki, as vice president. He also retired Chief of Staff General Sami Annan and Field Marshall Tantawi, his defense minister who headed SCAF for the 17-month transition period. Additionally, Morsi ordered the retirement of navy, air defense, and

---

[111] Ibid.

[112] AFP, "Egypt's Islamist-led parliament calls for expulsion of Israeli envoy" *Al Arabiya News,* March 12, 2012. http://english.alarabiya.net/articles/2012/03/12/200287.html (accessed September 2, 2012).

[113] Nathan Toronto, "Egypt's 'Coup-volution'" *Middle East Insights*, February 16, 2011.

air force commanders.[114] Now that Morsi has top military leaders who are loyal to him, he can gradually shift the armed forces to full civilian control.

President Morsi is placing other Muslim Brotherhood loyalists in top government posts. He replaced 50 editors of the government controlled media outlets and appointed new governors in many regions of the country.[115] Former Israeli ambassador to Egypt, Zvi Mazel, sees the Brotherhood methodically assuming total control of government institutions; those opposed to an Islamic regime have limited power to resist. Mazel argues that Morsi's current challenge is with the Mubarak era judiciary. The Supreme Constitutional Court could rule the Brotherhood Movement and FJP illegal and therefore invalidate the recent presidential and parliamentary elections. Morsi is working to limit the prerogatives of the court and retire senior justices appointed by Mubarak.[116] The Brotherhood's gradual and pragmatic rise to power has shown political shrewdness and organization. It used tensions between the conservative Salafists, liberal-secularists, and military leadership to its advantage to win the elections. Morsi and his FJP seem to be using the same gradual, pragmatic approach to consolidate political power.

The Economic Environment

Egyptian leaders face the staggering problem of bringing the Egyptian economy online with the rest of the developed world. A report published by the Institute of International Finance in May 2011 projected the economies of Egypt, Jordan, Lebanon, Morocco, Syria, and Tunisia to shrink by a collective 0.5 percent, reversing 4.4 percent growth in 2010. The growth forecast for the North African region as a whole has fallen from 4.5 percent in 2010 to less than 1 percent in

---

[114] Associated Press, "Egypt's president cancels amendments that gave military power, names vice president," *Fox News,* August 12, 2012. http://www.foxnews.com/world/2012/08/12/egypt-president-cancels-amendments-that-gave-military-power-names-vice/#ixzz23Mr373f3 (accessed September 23, 2012).

[115] Zvi Mazel, "Analysis: Brotherhood taking total control of Egypt" *The Jerusalem Post,* August 23, 2012. http://www.jpost.com/MiddleEast/Article.aspx?ID=282258 (accessed September 23, 2012).

[116] Ibid.

2011, according to the African Central Bank.[117] Although the report aggregates these figures by region, they reflect the general economic conditions in Egypt.

Egypt is the largest Arab country in demographic terms. Up to 60 percent of its population is under the age of 30. Economist Paul Rivlin argues Egypt's demographic transition would be a blessing instead of a curse if Mubarak had invested in private economic growth instead of a bloated, inefficient public sector, and social welfare programs.[118] Mubarak did invest in education, but as the working-age population and average education levels grew, there was no corresponding job growth. In 2005, Egyptian unemployment was around 10 to 12 percent. However, scholars estimate 30 to 40 percent unemployment among the younger, moderately educated workforce.[119] A large population of educated and economically frustrated young people created the conditions for the Egyptian revolt.

The main obstacle to change before 2011 was Egypt's authoritarian form of government. The regime maintained power by distributing income from rents (primarily oil exports, remittances, Suez Canal proceeds, and foreign aid). This created a patronage system that was unaccountable to the people. Economists Alan Richards and John Waterbury argue rents allowed Egypt to avoid thorough reform of its highly distorted pricing system and its structurally imbalanced labor market.[120] Rivlin claims public sector growth was favored over the private sector and international trade focused on an inefficient import substitution model. This created a political and economic equilibrium where there was little incentive for radical change, since it

---

[117] Ty McCormick, "The Arab Recession" *Foreign Policy,* July 22, 2011. http://www.foreignpolicy.com/articles/2011/07/22/the_arab_recession?page=full (accessed September 21, 2011).

[118] Rivlin, *Arab Economies in the Twenty-First Century*, 96, 129-131.

[119] Rivlin, *Arab Economies in the Twenty-First Century*, 102-105, Richards and Waterbury, *A Political Economy of the Middle East,* 133-141, and Knickmeyer, "The Arab World's Youth Army", 122. All three of these sources discuss the volatile, combined effects youth bulge, education and high unemployment have on the MENA region.

[120] Richards and Waterbury, *A Political Economy of the Middle East,* 17.

would threaten the stability of the regime. Rivlin acknowledged the only factors that could force change were domestic unrest of unemployed youth and a fall in rental income from oil.[121]

In the last 10 years, Egypt has gone from a net exporter to a net importer of oil. Egyptian oil production peaked in 1996. Exports began falling in 1997 and went negative in 2007.[122] High oil prices usually benefit the states of MENA; however, in Egypt's case prices aggravated economic conditions, as it had to import more oil each year to meet demand. As oil exports declined in Egypt, Mubarak accelerated economic reforms. In 2004, he appointed new ministers who reformed the exchange-rate system, reduced import tariffs, and reduced subsidies on fuel and electricity. Mubarak also reformed the banking sector, taxes, and public expenditures, and he privatized many state-owned firms.[123] Although these reforms were necessary to restructure Egypt's economy, they did not adequately alleviate Egypt's growing unemployment and social welfare problems.[124]

Since 1979, the U.S. has encouraged economic development in Egypt. From 1998 to 2003, Washington provided an average of $760 million in economic aid. In the last three years, this fell to $250 million.[125] In 2004, Egypt entered a politically contested trade agreement with the U.S. and Israel. This agreement set up eight Qualified Economic Zones (QIZs) that allowed Egypt to manufacture and export duty free to the U.S. as long as the goods contained a minimum of 11.7 percent Israeli value added share.[126] This allowed the expansion of industrial exports and the creation of much needed jobs. However, the economic benefits of the QIZs were slow in

---

[121] Rivlin, *Arab Economies in the Twenty-First Century*, 113. 293-295.

[122] Chris Martenson, "Egypt's Warning: Are you Listening?" *Chris Martenson.Com*, February 9, 2011. http://www.chrismartenson.com/blog/egypts-warning-are-you-listening/52575 (accessed September 24, 2011).

[123] Rivlin, *Arab Economies in the Twenty-First Century*, 114-116.

[124] Richards and Waterbury, *A Political Economy of the Middle East,* 17.

[125] See Table 1. U.S. Foreign Assistance to Egypt.

[126] Sharp, *Egypt in Transition,* 18.

coming. Many Egyptians were hostile to QIZs, since they benefited Israel. This reflects a general zero-sum mentality that whatever Israel gains, Egypt and Arabs in general lose.[127] Reinforcing this sentiment is the sale of natural gas to Israel through a pipeline in the Sinai. Egyptian authorities recently investigated businessmen with close ties to Mubarak for selling gas to Israel at steep discounts, costing the treasury $714 million in lost revenue. Some candidates supported the popular position of eliminating natural gas sales to Israel.[128] This hostility towards Israel has a direct impact on Egyptian stability and economic development.

Nasser's legacy of military control continues to play a significant role in the Egyptian economy. After sixty years, the military elite became entrenched in Egyptian economics. With Mubarak gone, SCAF continued to control the country. Military control poses yet another impediment to economic recovery. The military runs numerous enterprises. It enjoys tax exemptions, employs conscripted labor, and buys public land at below-market prices. Such distortions are likely to persist, since SCAF shielded its budget from public oversight and presidential control.[129] Complicating the military's economic entanglements is the security assistance relationship with the U.S. Vogelsang argues that the U.S. relationship helps protect the military's economic role, indirectly benefiting the Egyptian economy.[130] Morsi and the Brotherhood claim a popular mandate to eliminate the financial power of the military elite; however, the generals have mounted stiff resistance against such actions.[131] Gaining control over

---

[127] Rivlin, *Arab Economies in the Twenty-First Century*, 117-118. Richards and Waterbury also discuss the tendency for Muslim countries to be wary of economic dealings with non-Muslim countries. Richards and Waterbury, *A Political Economy of the Middle East*, 31.

[128] Sharp, *Egypt in Transition*, 10.

[129] McCormick, "The Arab Recession".

[130] Vogelsang, *U.S.-Egypt Security Cooperation after Egypt's January 2011 Revolution*, 4.

[131] Leila Fadel, "Muslim Brotherhood asserts its strength in Egypt with challenges to military" *The Washington Post,* March 25, 2012. http://www.washingtonpost.com/world/middle_east/muslim-brotherhood-asserts-its-strength-in-egypt-with-challenges-to-military/2012/03/21/gIQAJ9pmaS_story.html (accessed September 6, 2012).

the military budget will mark a full consolidation of power for Morsi and could threaten future U.S. security cooperation.

Local food and water scarcity and an unstable global food market are other underlying causes of Mubarak's overthrow. In the last two decades, three waves of food riots have jolted the North Africa region. The most recent was in 2008 when prices spiked before global recession reduced demand. Prices spiked again before the 2011 uprisings. The United Nations' Food and Agriculture Organization reported on 5 January that its worldwide food price index hit a record high in December, exceeding the 2008 peak.[132] A qualitative study by Marco Lagi, Karla Z. Bertrand, and Yaneer Bar-Yam supports the hypothesis that food prices are the precipitating condition for social unrest. They maintain that the 2011 Arab uprisings did not arise from long-standing political failings of the system, but from its perceived failure to provide essential food security.[133]

Another problem is the types of foods people consume in the region. Arab countries are the world's primary importers of cereal (a wheat product). Arab countries import around 60 million tons of cereal annually to feed 335 million people. Since there are a limited number of suppliers on the global cereal market, the region is vulnerable to global price fluctuations.[134] Several Arab governments maintain policies to sustain or subsidize local prices. These short-term reactions to manage sudden rises in wheat prices will not solve the structural conditions that fuel the global demand for staple foods. Moreover, urban development, rural migration, and repetitive

---

[132] Commodity Online, "Food crisis threatens import dependent Arab nations" *Commodity Online,* January 21, 2011. http://www.commodityonline.com/news/Food-crisis-threatens-import-dependent-Arab-nations-35836-3-1 html (accessed September 24, 2011).

[133] Marco Lagi, Karla Z. Bertran, and Yaneer Bar-Yam, "The Food Crises and Political Instability in North Africa and the Middle East" *Cornell University Library,* August 11, 2011, 2. http://arxiv.org/abs/1108.2455 (accessed August 17, 2011).

[134] Lahcen Achy, "Arab World: To Fight Off Hunger and Food Shortages, Governments Must Plan" *Carnegie Moscow Center,* November 11, 2010. http://carnegie.ru/publications/?fa=41906 (accessed September 25, 2011).

droughts have led to a reduction in the amount of arable land and a decrease in the global wheat supply.[135] The lack of affordable food is one of the most pressing concerns for the new Egyptian president.

Economic conditions in Egypt continued to deteriorate in 2011. Roughly, 200 families control 90 percent of Egypt's wealth. Many wealthy families fled the country after Mubarak's fall to avoid corruption investigations.[136] The Egyptian Finance Ministry sought up to $12 billion from the international community to address its balance of payments gap. Tourism, a $12.3 billion industry, dropped 40 percent as foreign vacationers chose more stable destinations.[137] Joblessness, up 3 percent in 2011, plagues Egypt. Some analysts remain hopeful that Egypt will return to pre-revolution growth levels, since the economic fundamentals of the economy have not changed.[138]

Although Egypt has benefited from its relationship with Washington since 1979, combined U.S. aid to Egypt has declined from $2.1 billion in 1998 to $1.55 billion in 2010.[139] Americans have enjoyed a robust trade relationship with Egypt. In 2010, there was an annual trade surplus of $4.5 billion benefiting the U.S. Although Egyptian officials have tried to negotiate a Free Trade Agreement with Washington, the U.S. has not moved forward on the issue.[140] As part of its outreach to the Muslim world the Obama Administration has promoted science, technology, and entrepreneurship programs in Egypt. However, these efforts only amount to about $110 million.[141] Compared to other sources, U.S. economic support is modest.

---

[135] Ibid.

[136] McCormick, "The Arab Recession".

[137] Sharp, *Egypt in Transition*, 10.

[138] McCormick, "The Arab Recession".

[139] Sharp, *Egypt in Transition*, 12. See Table 1.

[140] Ibid., 17.

[141] Ibid,, 15-16.

The current American political and economic environment may reduce aid even further as some politicians and lobbying groups call for an end to Egyptian aid.

Table 1. U.S. Foreign Assistance to Egypt

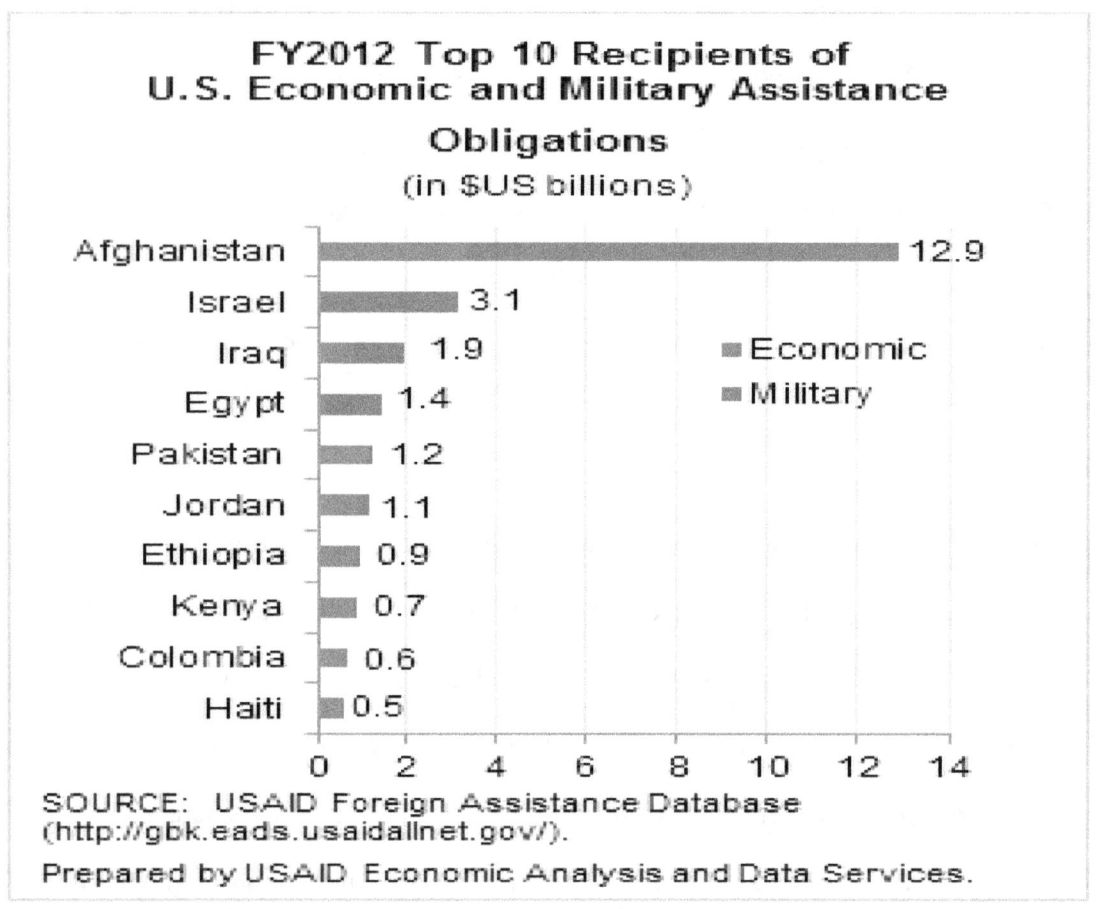

President Morsi has other sources of economic aid besides Washington. Before the parliamentary elections, Egypt received many pledges of support. The International Monetary Fund promised to provide $3 billion. The World Bank pledged up to $1 billion over 2011 and 2012 as well as $2.5 billion in loans for development projects, if the government met certain economic reforms. Saudi Arabia deposited $1 billion in Egypt's Central Bank in 2011 and guaranteed an additional $3 billion. Qatar promised to inject between $5 and $10 billion in

---

[142] Ibid., 18.

various projects, and G8 countries pledged loans of up to $5 billion through development banks.[143]

According to Egyptian economist Omar Abdel-Rahman, the Brotherhood will focus on serious threats to Egyptian stability first, like unemployment, social justice, and development. He foresees a Brotherhood government making strategic moves to distance itself from the West and concentrate on improving partnerships with countries like Turkey and Iran.[144] Shadi Hamid argues a Morsi government will pursue a more assertive and independent foreign policy, meaning more tension and disagreement with the U.S.[145] Even before the presidential election, the Brotherhood sought promises from the Gulf Cooperation Council for investment and public assistance. It received a promise of a $2 billion Islamic bond.[146] Morsi continues to improve relations with Saudi Arabia, Turkey, Iran, and China to decrease Egypt's dependence on the West.[147] These moves may significantly reduce the strategic influence and access the U.S. buys through aid to Egypt.

The Social Environment

Demographic changes, pro-democracy youth movements, food and water scarcity, internal religious tensions, and anti-Western sentiment shape the social environment in Egypt. Rapid population growth in the MENA region was a key factor underlying the 2011 Arab uprisings. Arab population growth rates are among the highest in the world. The population of the

---

[143] Ibid., 12.

[144] Egypt.com, "Egypt's MB to play a large economic role, experts claim" *Egypt.com,* August 2, 2011. http://news.egypt.com/english/permalink/26660 html (accessed September 6, 2012).

[145] Shadi Hamid, "Brother Number One." In *Islamists in a Changing Middle East*, by Foreign Policy, ed. Marc Lynch (n.p.: The FP Group, a division of the Washington Post Company, 2012), 102.

[146] Robert Springborg, "Egypt's cobra and mongoose" In *Islamists in a Changing Middle East*, by Foreign Policy, ed. Marc Lynch (n.p.: The FP Group, a division of the Washington Post Company, 2012), 60-61.

[147] Giorgio Cafiero, "Can Egypt Chart Its Own Course?" *Foreign Policy in Focus,* September 17, 2012. http://www.fpif.org/articles/can_egypt_chart_its_own_course (accessed September 30, 2012).

Arab world was 73 million in 1950. Now it is more than 333 million. The World Bank expects that to double again by 2050, to around 600 million.[148] This has created a substantial youth bulge in the Middle East. Egypt has the most people of any Arab country, with a population of over 80 million. This is 24 percent of the Arab world's population with a current annual increase of over one million. Its population has almost doubled over the last 30 years.[149] Sixty percent of Egyptians are under the age of 30. They are educated, literate, and many have university degrees, but they face unemployment rates of up to forty percent. These angry and unemployed young people are risking their lives and fueling political upheavals.[150]

The Mubarak regime was aware of this problem. Political scientists and development economists like Tarik Yousef, dean of the Dubai School of Government, have warned MENA governments of the coming youth bulge for years. They urged Arab leaders to harness the educated labor force flooding the market. This rising generation could have led to prosperity and growth as it has in other developing regions like Southeast Asia. Instead, Arab leaders invested little into economic development, resulting in an enormous generation of disillusioned and humiliated youth. In Mubarak's Egypt, many young people complained about corruption. Getting a job required connections to the country's ruling elite, a tribal leader, or a powerful businessman.[151] Ultimately, "dignity" drove the Egyptian revolution, the dignity of being able to put food on the table and provide for one's family.

One young Egyptian, Ahmed Maher, was instrumental in bringing down Mubarak. Educated and employed as a civil engineer, Maher was 31 years old in January of 2011.[152] In March of 2008, Maher created a Facebook page called April 6 Youth (A6Y) to support an

---

[148] Commodity Online, "Food crisis threatens import dependent Arab nations".

[149] Rivlin, *Arab Economies in the Twenty-First Century*, 96.

[150] Knickmeyer, "The Arab World's Youth Army", 122-123.

[151] Ibid., 124-125.

[152] Wolman, "The Instigators", 1.

upcoming workers' strike. Maher's online social media group grew to over 70,000 people and helped build massive turnout for the strike. The strike became an explosive street riot, attracting international media attention and embarrassing the regime. Although he suffered discrimination, arrest, and torture, Maher continued use his A6Y Facebook page to organize and demonstrate against Mubarak's regime.[153]

On June 6, 2010 Egyptian police beat a young man named Khalid Said to death. The senselessness of this killing sparked massive protests against police brutality. El-Baradei supported and participated in these protests. In response to the killing, Wael Ghonim, an Egyptian Google executive, anonymously started a Facebook page called "We Are All Khalid Said". Ghonim and Maher began to collaborate and organize a police day protest for January 25, 2011. Tension in Egypt rose throughout January due to a church bombing and the overthrow of Tunisian President Zine Ben Ali. Rumors spread of El-Baradei running for office. Facebook, Twitter, blogosphere, and cell phone chatter openly discussed revolution. On 25 January, tens of thousands of angry Egyptians marched on Tahrir Square. Although some called it a "leaderless" revolution, young activists like Maher and Ghonim played a considerable role in bringing down Mubarak. Even though most Egyptians did not have access to the internet, social media and cell phone technology were the tools used to organize the revolution.[154]

The young activists successfully overthrew a dictator, but Egypt's social challenges such as food and water shortages, poverty, internal religious tensions, and tensions with the U.S. and Israel continue to drive instability. The crucial issue facing Egypt's leaders is how to feed a rapidly growing population when water and food scarcity are becoming more severe. Lester Brown argues that the world is seeing the first collision between population growth and water

---

[153] Ibid., 3. In 2004 Maher became involved with the anti-Mubarak group Kefaya, Arabic for "enough". During the next four years, he continued to become involved in demonstrations against the regime.

[154] Ibid., 2.

43

supply at the regional level. He cites irreversible dropping grain production in the region. This causes most Arab countries to rely on grain imports and the global food market. The failure of Arab governments to mesh population, food, and water policies brings 10,000 more people to feed and less irrigation water with which to feed them each day.[155] According to the calculations of Lagi, Bertrand, and Bar-Yam, the underlying trend of increasing food prices will reach a threshold of instability between July 2012 and April 2013.[156]

Religious differences also complicate Egypt's society. About 90 percent of Egyptians are Sunni Muslim. However, within this group there are wide variations. Approximately 10 percent of Egyptians are Coptic Christians, the largest non-Muslim minority in the Arab world.[157] Although Muslims and Coptic Christians marched together to demand an end to Mubarak's reign, sectarian conflict between the religions increased after the revolution. In May 2011, an angry mob gathered in front of a Coptic church in Cairo, falsely believing the Copts were holding a convert to Islam against her will. The ensuing violence claimed the lives of six Muslims and six Copts, wounded 200 others, and burned two churches.[158]

Historically, Egypt's leaders exploit sectarian tensions to consolidate political power. Since the revolution, some Salafist leaders sought to exploit sectarian divides to further their Islamist ideals.[159] In October 2011, the Army responded to street violence between Coptic

---

[155] Lester Brown, "The Great Food Crisis of 2011" *Foreign Policy,* January 10, 2011. http://www.foreignpolicy.com/articles/2011/01/10/the_great_food_crisis_of_2011?page=full (accessed September 24, 2011).

[156] Lagi, Bertran, and Bar-Yam, "The Food Crises and Political Instability in North Africa and the Middle East", 5.

[157] Central Intelligence Agency, *World Fact Book,* September 13, 2012. https://www.cia.gov/library/publications/the-world-factbook/geos/eg.html (accessed September 30, 2012).

[158] Michael Wahid Hanna, "Sectarianism Stalks Egypt" In *Islamists in a Changing Middle East,* by Foreign Policy, ed. Marc Lynch (n.p.: The FP Group, a division of the Washington Post Company, 2012), 64.

[159] Ibid., 65-66.

Christian Egyptians and Salafists. This clash claimed the lives of 24 protesters.[160] The

empowerment of Islamists has many concerned for the welfare of Christians. An Egyptian court

recently sentenced a Coptic teacher to six years in prison for insulting Islam and defaming

President Morsi on his Facebook page. Salafists outside the court building tried to attack the

defendant, threatening to kill his family and burn Christian houses.[161] These incidents indicate the

underlying sectarian tensions in Egyptian society.

Egypt's Islamist groups trace their roots back to al-Banna and the foundation of the

Muslim Brotherhood. After Nasser era suppression, the Brotherhood reemerged during Anwar

Sadat's presidency as a movement committed to nonviolent political participation. Disagreements

over the nonviolent, gradual approach caused many groups to split with the Brotherhood. These

groups drew inspiration from the writings of Sayyid Qutb. Imprisoned during the Nasser era,

Qutb's fundamentalist tracts endorsed a violent takeover of power.[162] One of the pro-violence

groups that emerged from the Brotherhood in 1979 was the Society of Struggle (*Jama'at al-*

Jihad). Ayman al-Zawahiri, Omar Abdel Rhaman, and Abbud al-Zumur were founding leaders of

al-Jihad. Disillusioned by the Brotherhood's passivity and the American brokered peace deal

with Israel, the group assassinated Sadat in 1981. In retaliation, Mubarak repressed the group, and

it divided into factions. Mubarak exiled Rhaman to the U.S. where he planned the 1993 World

Trade Center bombing; al-Zawahiri led a new group in Afghanistan where he joined with Osama

---

[160] Vogelsang, *U.S.-Egypt Security Cooperation after Egypt's January 2011 Revolution*, 67.

[161] Said Shehata, "The misery of Copts in Egypt " *Ahram Online,* October 2, 2012. http://english.ahram.org.eg/NewsContentP/4/54512/Opinion/The-misery-of-Copts-in-Egypt--.aspx (accessed October 2, 2012).

[162] David Zedan, "Radical Islam in Egypt" In *Revolutionaries and Reformers: Contemporary Islamist Movements in the Middle East*, ed. Barry Rubin (Albany: State University of New York, 2003), 11-12.

bin-Laden's al-Qaida organization; al-Zumur formed the Egyptian Islamic Group (IG) and was later imprisoned.[163]

In 1997, the IG abandoned armed activism as a tool for political change. Released from prison in March 2011, Abbud al-Zumur continues to lead IG, rejects violence, participates in elections, and promotes peaceful coexistence with Copts. However, he also maintains the IG's conservative Islamist ideals. Since the revolution, the IG has held several rallies in front of the U.S. embassy demanding the release of their inspirational "godfather", Omar Rhaman, imprisoned for his role in the 1993 World Trade Center bombing.[164] Appealing to popular Islamist sentiment, Morsi has pledged to seek the release of Rhaman from U.S. custody.[165]

The IG falls under the umbrella of Egypt's Salafist groups who uphold a strict interpretation of Islam that emulates the ways of the first three generations of Muslims. Many Salafis have developed a distinctive appearance and code of personal behavior, including untrimmed beards for men and the niqab for women. Prior to the 2011 revolution, Salafis rejected democratic political participation as contrary to sharia law. After Mubarak's fall, they were eager to be part of the system. By participating in the current political process, they hope to ensure Egypt's new constitution imposes sharia law. Salafi spokesmen emphasize modest political aims and practical solutions to economic and social problems. However, some Salafi scholars like Sheikh Hassan Abu Asahbal see the revolution eventually leading to a dominant Muslim caliphate. "It's Allah's plan for us to build one country in the Muslim world and rule the world,"

---

[163] Ibid., 13, 18-19.

[164] Omar Ashour, "Egypt's Democratic Jihadists?" In *Islamists in a Changing Middle East*, by Foreign Policy, ed. Marc Lynch (n.p.: The FP Group, a division of the Washington Post Company, 2012), 67-69.

[165] David Kirkpatrick, "Egypt's New Leader Takes Oath, Promising to Work for Release of Jailed Terrorist" *The New York Times,* June 20, 2012. http://www.nytimes.com/2012/06/30/world/middleeast/morsi-promises-to-work-for-release-of-omar-abdel-rahman html?_r=1 (accessed September 6, 2012).

he claims.[166] Similar to the Brotherhood, there is a generational divide within Salafist organizations. Many Salafi sheikhs opposed the Arab uprisings and Bouazizi's suicide as un-Islamic. The younger generation rejected the sheikhs' guidance and joined the revolution. These divisions made it difficult for Salafis to present a clear, unified message.[167] Salafist influence, along with the Brotherhood, will weigh heavily in Egypt's future.

One of the key differences between the Muslim Brotherhood and Salafists is their timetable for implementing sharia. Both groups agree on the need; however, the Brotherhood sees it happening gradually over decades so that society is prepared. Political spokesmen for the FJP emphasize the need for a constitution that preserves the rights of all citizens, regardless of religion. Safalists, however, want to implement sharia quickly. Ibrahim AbdulRahman, a Safalist spokesman, states, "one of the primary major goals is to implement sharia at the nearest possible opportunity".[168] The Salafist's immediate approach reflects their historical willingness to use violence to further political goals.

Since the 2011 revolution, political and social tensions between the U.S. and Egypt have significantly increased. During the latter half of 2011, SCAF attempted to discredit the liberal-secular activists by portraying them as American agents for accepting U.S. technical assistance. Under Mubarak, United States Agency for International Development's (USAID) democracy and governance programs were restricted. However, after the 2011 revolution, USAID's Cairo office began soliciting grant proposals from Egyptian nongovernmental organizations (NGOs). Although the State Department proclaimed the programs were politically neutral, Egyptian officials saw them as U.S. interference in Egyptian elections. SCAF accused the Obama

---

[166] Lauren Bohn, "Inside Egypt's Salafis" In *Islamists in a Changing Middle East*, by Foreign Policy, ed. Marc Lynch (n.p.: The FP Group, a division of the Washington Post Company, 2012), 74-75.

[167] Ibid., 75.

[168] Sarah A Topol, "Egypt's Salafi Surge" In *Islamists in a Changing Middle East*, by Foreign Policy, ed. Marc Lynch (n.p.: The FP Group, a division of the Washington Post Company, 2012), 84.

administration of unlawfully funneling money to unregistered foreign democracy assistance organizations.[169] In December 2011, SCAF raided NGO offices and prevented American NGO workers from leaving the country. U.S. lawmakers threatened to cut off aid if SCAF did not let the NGO workers leave. When SACF lifted the travel ban, the Brotherhood-led parliament debated refusing U.S. aid and removing the military-appointed government for giving in to American pressure.[170] Although these events strained U.S - Egyptian relations, they demonstrated SCAFs ability to use anti-American sentiment to diminish the power of liberal activists.

A 2011 BBC country-rating poll indicated that only 26 percent of Egyptians held positive views of the United States.[171] It is likely that this sentiment fell even more in 2012. After Morsi's election, many liberal politicians developed anti-American conspiracy theories to explain why Islamists prevailed. One former presidential candidate claimed that the Obama administration was backing the Brotherhood so it could then use the establishment of Egyptian theocracy as a pretext for an Iraq-style invasion.[172] On September 11, 2012, angry over a U.S. produced film that insulted the Prophet Mohammad, Egyptian protesters scaled the walls of the U.S. Embassy, then tore down and burned the American flag.[173] The intensity and duration of these protests indicate the difficult challenge Washington will have in maintaining its interests in the MENA region.

Egyptian-Israeli tensions are even worse than Egyptian-U.S. tensions. Although Egypt and Israel have maintained their treaty agreements, Israel has voiced concerns over the deteriorating security situation in the Sinai. In response to militant attacks in July 2011 on the

---

[169] Sharp, *Egypt in Transition*, 2-3.

[170] Hamid, "Brother Number One.", 101.

[171] BBC World Service, *Views of US Continue to Improve in 2011 BBC Country Rating Poll,* Opinion Poll (London: BBC World Service, 2011), 8.

[172] Shadi Hamid, "It Ain't Just a River in Egypt" *Foreign Policy,* July 30, 2012. http://www.foreignpolicy.com/articles/2012/07/30/it_ain_t_just_a_river_in_egypt?page=0,0 (accessed September 30, 2012).

[173] Tamim Elyan, "Egyptians angry at film scale U.S. embassy walls" *Reuters,* September 11, 2012. http://www.reuters.com/article/2012/09/11/us-egypt-usa-protest-idUSBRE88A11N20120911 (accessed September 30, 2012).

natural gas pipeline that runs between Egypt and Israel, Egypt deployed 1,000 troops to the Sinai. Israel agreed to this deployment in accordance with the 1979 treaty. In August 2011, a Gazan terrorist cell traversed the Sinai into Israel and attacked Israeli vehicles and soldiers. Israel responded with aircraft, killing five terrorists and five Egyptian solders in the crossfire when militants fled across the border. Egypt demanded an apology and compensation from Israel as thousands of protestors demonstrated outside the Israeli embassy in Cairo. The protestors burned Israeli flags and demanded the government expel the ambassador and close the embassy.[174] These attacks on Israel's embassy reveal the violent passions that can erupt in Egypt due to frustration over long-simmering Israeli-Palestinian issues.

This tension between Egypt and Israel along the Sinai border region continued to flare up in 2012. In March, violence escalated in Gaza as Israeli air strikes targeted militant leaders and Hamas rockets targeted Israeli settlements, claiming over 25 lives. In response, Egypt's parliament called for the expulsion of the Israeli ambassador and the recall of Egypt's ambassador to Israel. [175] In April 2012, Egypt unilaterally ended its natural gas export contract with Israel. Although explained as the termination of a legal business dispute, the Mubarak era gas deal is unpopular with many Egyptians. Militants in the Sinai have attacked the gas pipeline at least 14 times since January 2011.[176] Tensions in the Gaza and Sinai region will likely continue to flare up and possibly escalate. This will put increasing pressure on a popularly elected Islamist government to cancel the Camp David Peace Accords.

---

[174] Sharp, *Egypt in Transition*, 1.

[175] AFP, "Egypt's Islamist-led parliament calls for expulsion of Israeli envoy" *Al Arabiya News,* March 12, 2012. http://english.alarabiya.net/articles/2012/03/12/200287.html (accessed September 2, 2012).

[176] Ahmed Feteha, "Egypt cancels gas deal; Israeli minister warns of 'implications' for Camp David Accords" *Ahram Online,* April 23, 2012. http://english.ahram.org.eg/NewsContent/3/12/39931/Business/Economy/Egypt-cancels-gas-deal;-Israeli-minister-warns-of-.aspx (accessed September 30, 2012).

The Military Environment

Since 1979, the Camp David Peace Accords have overshadowed the security environment in Egypt. Egyptian Islamist outrage over the peace deal cost Sadat his life in 1981. A key provision of the Accords was the withdrawal of Israeli forces behind the 1947 international boundary (which left Gaza within Israel). The agreement called for UN peacekeepers to monitor a buffer zone in the Sinai; however, the Security Council would not authorize UN participation. In 1982, the U.S., with other supporting countries, formed the Multinational Force and Observers (MFO) to monitor implementation and adherence to the Accords.[177]

MFO monitors a buffer zone on the Egyptian side of the border. It consists of land, air, and naval forces from twelve contributing nations. As of September 2011, MFO numbered 1,656 personnel.[178] Recent violence against Egyptian border guards in the Sinai is affecting the MFO mission. With support from Israel, Egypt has moved large numbers of armored vehicles and troops into the demilitarized, MFO-patrolled zone to crack down on lawlessness and terrorism. In August 2012, militants attacked a police checkpoint that had an MFO position nearby.[179] This escalation of violence in the Sinai will continue to challenge the MFO mission and intensify tensions between Egypt and Israel.

As part of the 1979 Camp David Accords, Washington has maintained a robust military-to-military relationship with Egypt. Over the last ten years, Egypt has received approximately

---

[177] Robert R. Kiser, *The History of Peacekeeping in the Sinai Desert 1959-2002,* MMAS Thesis (Fort Leavenworth, KS: U.S Army Command and General Staff College, 2003), 72.

[178] Multinational Force and Observers, *Multinational Force and Observers.* 2012. http://www.mfo.org/index.php (accessed February 13, 2012). The U.S. provides the largest contingent with the Task Force Headquarters element, a support battalion and an infantry battalion. Columbia and Fiji each provide an infantry battalion as well.

[179] Reuters, "Egypt Sinai peacekeepers deny they came under fire" *Reuters,* August 12, 2012. http://www.reuters.com/article/2012/08/12/us-egypt-sinai-attack-idUSBRE87A0MD20120812 (accessed October 5, 2012).

$1.3 billion annually in military aid.[180] Recent U.S. appropriations have tied aid to enhanced border security programs in the Sinai, and the expectation that Egypt continues its obligations under the Egypt-Israel Peace Accords.[181] Military aid pays for new equipment, upgrades to existing equipment, and support and maintenance contracts.[182] One example is the coproduced M1A1 Abrams Main Battle Tank program, which began in 1988 with Egypt planning to acquire 1,200 tanks.[183] This military aid has produced an Egyptian military that is substantially dependent on the U.S.

Egypt receives additional support through Excess Defense Articles from the Pentagon worth hundreds of millions of dollars annually. Egyptian officers also participate in the International Military and Education Training (IMET) program amounting to roughly $1.4 million annually. The IMET program facilitates U.S.-Egyptian military cooperation over the long term. Egypt and the U.S. also participate in joint exercises fostering interoperability. Bright Star is a biannual, multinational training exercise co-hosted by the U.S. and Egyptian land forces. Eagle Salute is a joint maritime training exercise conducted annually in the Red Sea.[184] However, Egypt has not conducted these exercises since the 2011 revolution.

The billions spent on security cooperation with Egypt has served U.S. interests. Strategically, it has maintained Egyptian-Israeli peace and provided access to the Suez Canal and Egyptian airspace. Operationally, it endeavors to achieve key DOD goals of interoperability and

---

[180] See Table 1, U.S. Foreign Assistance to Egypt.

[181] Sharp, *Egypt in Transition*, 1-2.

[182] Government Accountability Office. *State and DOD Need to Assess How the Foreign Military Financing Program for Egypt Achieves U.S. Foreign Policy and Security Goals,* Security Assistance, GAO-06-437 (Washington D.C.: United States Government Accountability Office, April 2006), 2. According to this report, U.S. military aid pays for 80% of Egypt's acquisitions. Major purchases over the life of the program are 36 Apache helicopters, 220 F-16 aircraft and 880 M1A1 tanks along with the training and maintenance programs to support these systems.

[183] Sharp, *Egypt in Transition*, 16.

[184] Ibid., 16-17.

modernization.[185] The relationship has benefited the U.S. in other ways. Toronto argues that there is circumstantial evidence to suggest that, "the IMET program contributed to the Egyptian Army's restraint" during the 2011 uprising. He reasons that Egyptian Army officers who studied at U.S. schools would have been in positions of influence during the anti-Mubarak protests.[186] The fact that Defense Secretary Gates and Admiral Mullen had direct contact with Egypt's Defense Minister, Field Marshal Tantawi, and Army Chief of Staff, Lieutenant General Anan, during the 2011 uprisings strengthens Toronto's argument.[187] This demonstrates the value of the U.S.-Egyptian military relationship, which is arguably the best leverage the U.S. has to influence Egypt.

Since 1979, the U.S. has spent billions of dollars on security assistance to Egypt, but there are questions over whether it has been effective in developing Egyptian war fighting capacity and interoperability. Toronto argues that U.S. military aid has had little visible effect on Egyptian military capacity.[188] Analyzing Egyptian military performance during the 1991 Gulf War, Kenneth Pollack states that U.S. equipment, doctrine, and training have done little to improve Egyptian military effectiveness. Pollack asserts the Egyptians fight well in set-piece offensives and static defensive operations; however, they fail miserably when conducting operations with limited planning time or fighting maneuver battles.[189] During training, U.S. advisors observed over-centralization, lack of higher echelon or combined arms training,

---

[185] Government Accountability Office. *State and DOD Need to Assess*, 3-4.

[186] Nathan Toronto, *Active Inaction: Interagency Security Assistance to Egypt,* Interagency Occasional Paper No. 6 (Fort Leavenworth, Kansas: CGSC Foundation Press, November 2011), 12.

[187] Josh Rogin, "Gates and Mullen in close contact with Egyptian military" *Foreign Policy,* February 11, 2011. http://thecable.foreignpolicy.com/posts/2011/02/11/gates_and_mullen_in_close_contact_with_egyptian_mi litary (accessed September 30, 2012).

[188] Toronto, *Active Inaction*, 1.

[189] Pollack, *Arabs at War*, 139-142, 148-147. During Operation Desert Storm, Pollack states U.S. planners had more confidence in the Egyptians than other Arab contingents; however, the Egyptian led task force moved at a glacial pace against almost no Iraqi resistance, showed no initiative or flexibility and was unable to reach its planned objectives.

compartmentalization of information, exaggerated or false reporting, scripted training exercises, and little capacity to handle or maintain sophisticated equipment. Egypt's inability to perform preventive maintenance or proper repairs forces it to rely on U.S. contracts for depot level maintenance.[190] All of these factors leave Egypt with a military that has little offensive capability.

Instead of developing a capable military focused on external threats, Mubarak maintained armed forces that supported Egypt's economy, protected the regime, and mitigated internal threats. Even with U.S. military assistance and equipment, Mubarak did not completely retire obsolete Soviet-supplied armaments. Keeping the equipment meant keeping the labor to manage it. This allowed the Egyptian military to fulfill one of its domestic roles, as an employer in a jobs-starved economy.[191] Although Mubarak attempted to improve military professionalism, political connections, rather than competence or experience, increasingly determined senior command positions.[192] Ayoob asserts that so much of the energy of Arab armies is devoted to the task of regime preservation that it detracts gravely from their war-fighting capacity. He cites the defeats inflicted by Israel on Egyptian, Syrian, and Jordanian armies in 1967 and on Egyptian and Syrian armies in 1973 as examples.[193]

The current environment presents an Egyptian military enmeshed in its economy and national politics, dependent on U.S. aid, with limited power projection or offensive capabilities. This would make it likely for a pragmatic Brotherhood government to use conventional military force primarily in a defensive role. In a conflict with Israel, Egypt is likely to use diplomacy and asymmetric means to achieve strategic aims.

---

[190] Pollack, *Arabs at War*, 142-145.

[191] Vogelsang, *U.S.-Egypt Security Cooperation after Egypt's January 2011 Revolution*, 3.

[192] Pollack, *Arabs at War*, 138-139.

[193] Ayoob, "The Tyrant is Dead, But What About His Tyranny?", 212.

Comparison and Synthesis of Operational Variables

The purpose of this study is to anticipate the potential of a new "Suez" type crisis in light of the recent Egyptian revolution. While there are many important variables to compare between the two periods, not all of them are relevant. Therefore, this section focuses on revolutionary variables within Egypt that had a causal relationship to the 1956 Suez Crisis or would have a causal relationship to a future crisis in the Sinai. For the purposes of comparison, this section refers to the 1950s environment as the "Nasser era" and the current environment as the "Muslim Brotherhood era".

In comparing the current the current revolutionary environment in Egypt with the environment in the 1950s and the 1956 Suez Crisis, a pattern of five common revolutionary phases emerge (See Table 2). Both revolutionary phases began with a pre-revolution phase that set the conditions for uprising. These conditions lead to the revolutionary moment when forces coalesce to overthrow the old regime. After the initial euphoria and triumph of tearing down the old order, different political groups struggled for power and influence in the new order. One group with a recognizable leader emerged and worked to consolidate control over state power. Once internal control was established, the Nasser regime turned to regional and global issues that would win broad popular support, leading to the 1956 Suez Crisis. If the Brotherhood follows this pattern, Western leaders can expect renewed Egyptian-Israeli conflict and the eruption of another crisis in the Sinai region.

Table 2. Causal Pattern of Egyptian Revolutions Leading to a Suez or Sinai Crisis

	1950s Nasser Era	2010s Muslim Brotherhood Era
Pre-Revolution	-Dysfunctional Parlimentary system & corruption -Liberaism, Islamism and communism -Economic and social transition -Defeat and dissilusionment from 1948 Arab-Israeli war -Anti-zionism, anti-imperialism -Calls for social justice	-Weakening authoritarian system, corruption & police brutality -Liberalism & Islamism -Youth bulge, stagnant economic condtions, food shortages, educated populace and internet technology -Anti-American and anti-Israeli sentiment
Revolutionary Moment	July 23, 1952 -Coup by Free Officer movement -Monarchy overthrown -Purge of old guard aristocratic leadership	Jan 25, 2011 -April 6th Youth led protest movement -Coalition of Liberal democracts and Islamists protest in Tahrir Square -Egyptian Army protects protestors -Mubarak falls after two weeks of massive protests
Post-Revolution Contest for Power	-Nasser rises to the top of Free Officer movement -Naqib as a figurehead -Form Command Council of the Revolution -Nasser tries to co-opt Brotherhood and communist parties	-SCAF control of transitional government -Parliamentary elections: Muslim Brotherhood wins a majority followed by Salafist coalition -Presdential Elections: Rise of Mohammed Morsi -SCAF attempts to limit presidential power
Post-Revolution Consolidation of Power	-March 1954 Crisis -Nasser consolidates power over Wafd, Muslim Brotherhood and communist parties	-June 2012 - Morsi elected president -Freedom and Justice Party currently consolidating power over military and judicial institutions
New Regime Exerts Regional and Global Influence	Deterioration of US-Egyptian Relations + Egypt signs Soviet Arms deal + US withdraws funding for the Aswan Dam = 1956 Suez Crisis	Anticipated events: *Deterioration of US-Egyptian security cooperation relationship* *+ US withdrawl of foreign aid* *+ Abrogation of the Camp David Accords* *= New crisis in the Sinai*

Pre-Revolution

A dysfunctional parliamentary system, a corrupt monarch, and British occupation characterized the pre-revolution phase of the Nasser era. The Brotherhood and various communist movements opposed the ruling establishment. Egypt suffered from economic stagnation, rising prices, and high unemployment. These economic conditions drove social changes as Egypt was transitioning from an aristocratic agrarian society to an industrialized urban society with a rising middle class. Egypt's defeat in 1948 disillusioned military leaders and the populace in general.

Passions of anti-Zionism directed toward Israel, anti-imperialism directed toward British

occupation, and anti-aristocratic ideals of social justice motivated most Egyptians. These

conditions drove Nasser's Free Officer movement to take action on July 23, 1952.

A weak parliament, an authoritarian, military dominated dictatorship, and an unpopular

strategic relationship with the U.S. and Israel characterized the pre-revolutionary environment of

the Muslim Brotherhood era. Movements like A6Y organized anti-government protests online

and in the streets to challenge Mubarak's control. Egypt's bulging population of educated youth

pushed for change through both liberal democratic movements and conservative Islamist

movements. Their demands centered on economic conditions, food prices, social justice, police

brutality, and the corruption of Mubarak's regime. El-Baradei inspired these youth with his

demands for democracy. Mubarak and his military leaders were committed to the 1979 Camp

David Accords and a strategic relationship with Washington. However, average Egyptians

resented the peace treaty with Israel and were distrustful of U.S interference in the Middle East.

The December 2010 uprisings in Tunisia provided the spark that ignited revolutionary Egyptian

passions in January 2011.

Revolutionary Moment

In 1952, Nasser's Free Officer movement took advantage of political weakness in Egypt

by taking control of the government ministries by force. The junta demanded that King Farouk

appoint General Nagib as prime minister and then forced the king to abdicate. The 23 July coup

was an unexpected blow to the ruling elite, but the Free Officers drew strong support from a

younger generation. Although diverse liberal democratic, Islamist, and communist movements

made up this younger generation, they all had grown disaffected from the country's political

leaders. While they supported the Free Officer junta, they did so believing the Free Officers

promises to purge the old political leadership, implement reforms, reestablish parliamentary government, and relinquish power. Nasser saw his coup as an inspiration for a popular movement; however, it was not long before the different political interests of the various parties disrupted the unity of his revolution.

On January 25, 2011, socially active Egyptian youth groups led by A6Y organized a massive protest. Exceeding expectations, the protesters drew in tens of thousands of protesters to Tahrir Square. They drew popular support across generational and political lines. Youth leaders of the Brotherhood joined in to support the secular movement. Their ability to organize and provide social services allowed the crowds of protesters to remain in Tahrir Square for over two weeks. Mubarak called in the Egyptian Army; however, the Army leadership refused to use lethal force to disperse the protesters. Egypt's military-dominated leadership realized that Mubarak would have to go in order to restore stability. On 11 February, Mubarak resigned and turned control of the government over to a military council. SCAF announced its transitional government would oversee new elections and a constitutional revision to give Egypt a civilian led democratic government. This opened the door for Egypt's diverse political factions to organize parties and contest for power.

Post-Revolution Contest for Power

Nasser's Free Officer junta installed General Nagib as a figurehead leader, purged old guard leadership, and instituted land reforms that limited the power of the aristocracy. He believed this would unify Egypt's factionalized parties. Instead, the competing interests of Islamists, communists, old guard aristocrats, and young liberal progressives struggled for power and threatened to tear the new government apart. In January 1953, Nasser formed the CCR and banned all political parties except the Brotherhood. He relied on the military and the Brotherhood's influence and organization to establish his base of power. Nasser was wary of the Brotherhood's pervasive influence, but his Free Officers had close ties to its leadership and Nasser believed he could co-opt them into maintaining his regime. The Free Officers tried to maintain the impression that once reforms were completed and Egypt was stable they would return control to a civilian government. However, the more they engaged in power politics, the more entrenched the CCR became.

Soon after Mubarak's fall, a power struggle along ideological, religious, and social lines developed. Three primary groups contended in this power struggle. SCAF tried to peacefully transition power to an elected civilian government, while ensuring the military's economic benefits and influence over foreign policy remained intact. Although initially skeptical about getting involved in democratic politics, Islamist movements capitalized on the revolutionary fervor in order to ensure sharia law would dominate the new Egyptian state. The more moderate Brotherhood reached out to liberal-secular groups and worked closely with SCAF to build a broad base of support. The conservative Salafists formed a coalition with a broad rural base of support. The final group was the pro-democracy protesters supported by liberal-secular parties. Playing SCAF, Salafists, and liberals against each other, the Brotherhood's FJP steadily gained majorities in parliamentary and presidential elections, ending with Mohamed Morsi gaining the presidency.

Post-Revolution Consolidation of Power

Throughout 1953 and early 1954, the Free Officer's regime was challenged from all sides. In January 1954, the Brotherhood and a faction within the army began supporting President Nagib, who was gaining popularity and power independent of the Free Officer junta. This caused the CCR to outlaw the Brotherhood and arrest its leaders. The next month the CCR denounced Nagib as a tyrant and ousted him. In March these actions unleashed opposition forces into a mass movement calling for the dismissal of the CCR and a return to civilian control. Initially the CCR agreed to step aside. However, this emboldened opposition leaders into revealing themselves so that state sponsored mob violence and coercion could silence the opposition before it could organize. Nasser then reasserted CCR control and "restored order". The "March Crisis" marked a turning point for the CCR as Nasser consolidated power and asserted control over the army, press, professional associations, labor unions, and universities. In October 1954, Nasser secured

the withdrawal of all British forces and survived an alleged Brotherhood assassination attempt.

These events secured popular domestic political support for Nasser and allowed him to focus

externally.

Currently, although focused on resolving Egypt's economic and social crisis, Morsi's

government is gradually consolidating state power under FJP control. He is placing loyalists in

top government posts, influencing a constitutional revision, and deflecting a challenge from a

Mubarak era judiciary. He has replaced top military commanders without any major resistance. If

he can impose full control over the military, he will have the ability to implement a Brotherhood

oriented foreign policy agenda. Robert Springborg of the Naval Postgraduate School argues that

the Brotherhood will move against the military simultaneously from the bottom and top. The

Brotherhood has real power and many supporters within the military and security service that can

influence from the bottom.[194] With the presidency and parliament now under its influence, the

Brotherhood is steadily positioning members and sympathizers in positions of authority.

New Regime Exerts Regional and Global Influence

With opposition suppressed and a popular mandate, Nasser began to support the pan-

Arab nationalist movement and Palestinian resistance in Israel. In 1955, he signed a treaty ending

British military occupation of the Canal Zone. Israeli retaliation against partisan raids led Nasser

to block the Tiran straights and make an arms deal with the Soviets. Favoring Arab

fragmentation, Israel, France, and Britain saw Nasser as their main threat. The U.S. initially

supported Nasser's regime and agreed to fund the Aswan High Dam project, which promised to

reinvigorate Egypt's economy. However, British influence and Nasser's turn to the Soviets led

Eisenhower to revoke funding for the dam in July 1956. A week later Nasser nationalized the

---

[194] Springborg, "Egypt's cobra and mongoose", 60.

Suez Canal, leading to war with Britain, France, and Israel in October. The crisis ended with Britain, France, and Israel withdrawing to pre-conflict borders. Although militarily the Egyptian forces were close to defeat, diplomatically Nasser emerged as a hero in the pan-Arab struggle against colonialism and Zionism.

Currently, Morsi's new Egyptian government is consolidating its control and reaching out to new global and regional partners. Although Morsi's outreach to Saudi Arabia, China, and others is primarily to gain economic support, he may also be looking for ways to eliminate Egypt's dependence on U.S. security assistance. Today both countries have a strategic interest in maintaining the military-to-military relationship; however, systemic tensions are making this relationship tenuous. Recent anti-American protests in the region are bringing this security cooperation relationship into question in Egyptian and American domestic politics. If either party terminates this relationship, the potential for renewed conflict between Egypt and Israel will increase significantly.

In 2011, journalist Brian Dabbs argued that a Brotherhood government would moderate its policy when in power and not do away with the Camp David Peace Accords or deep-rooted security cooperation with America.[195] Dabbs' assumption that U.S. influence will keep Egypt from going to war with Israel is valid until U.S. security assistance and economic aid stops. Instead of a deep-rooted alliance, there is a tenuous quid pro quo agreement that is under stress from all sides.

---

[195] Brian Dabbs, "Muslim Brotherhood No Threat to Egypt's Israel Policy" *World Politics Review,* July 21, 2011. http://www.worldpoliticsreview.com/articles/9542/muslim-brotherhood-no-threat-to-egypts-israel-policy (accessed September 6, 2012). Full quote from Dabbs: The deep-rooted U.S.-Egyptian political and security alliance and Egypt's peace treaty with Israel do not only serve American interests in the region, however. Should the Muslim Brotherhood be in a position to spearhead policy in the future, the group is not likely to confront the military on such an issue. Abolishing peace with Israel would strip the military of that aid and usher in further international isolation. For such reasons, leading figures in the Brotherhood's recently legalized political arm, the Freedom and Justice Party, claim the peace treaty will stay intact.

The security cooperation relationship is the primary means of influence the U.S. has with Egypt. Egyptian defense acquisitions as well as contracted training and maintenance support depend on U.S. funding. This gives the U.S. some degree of influence with the Egyptian government; however, this leverage is limited and fragile. Toronto argues,

> Developing the U.S.–Egypt military-to-military relationship is no guarantee of influence, but one thing is certain: if the U.S. drastically reduces its engagement with Egypt now, then its ability to influence future events will definitely be reduced, and the U.S. does not have very much influence in Egypt today. [196]

Due to the recent anti-American demonstrations in the MENA region, there was an effort in the U.S. Senate to cut all foreign aid to Egypt, Libya, and Pakistan. Although the bill was overwhelmingly defeated, proponents claimed that up to 80 percent of Americans support reducing foreign aid.[197] If the regional situation continues to deteriorate, Washington may give in to domestic pressure to reduce aid to Egypt. This would sever U.S. ties to the Egyptian military and force the Brotherhood administration to turn somewhere else for military support. Similar to the 1950s when Nasser exploited U.S.-Soviet tensions to his benefit, Morsi will likely utilize Western tensions with Iran, China, and Russia to his advantage.

Additionally, a popularly elected Islamist government will not be inclined to maintain peace with Israel. If Egypt becomes truly democratic, popular sentiments will move the country away from U.S. interests and toward war with Israel. Princeton University professor David Bell discounts the near-term possibility of Egypt's revolution turning into a radical Islamic movement like the one in Iran in 1979. However, he asserts that if the new government cannot deliver serious social and economic reforms, then a far more radical revolutionary movement may

---

[196] Toronto, *Active Inaction*, 13.

[197] W. James Antle, "Senate overwhelmingly rejects foreign aid cuts for Egypt, Libya and Pakistan" *The Daily Caller,* September 23, 2012. http://dailycaller.com/2012/09/23/senate-overwhelmingly-rejects-foreign-aid-cuts-for-egypt-libya-and-pakistan/ (accessed September 23, 2012).

develop, especially if a charismatic leader emerges.[198] Morsi may not be the charismatic leader Nasser was, but if he focuses internal economic and social discontent against the U.S. and Israel, he will win broad popular support.

In a pure democracy, the popular passions of the people will likely determine a country's direction. Using the example of the French Revolution in 1973, Carl von Clausewitz described the resources and vigorous efforts that a nation can mobilize for war when the passions of the people become involved.[199] The recent anti-American upheaval in Egypt and throughout the MENA region demonstrates what can happen when the religious passions of Muslims become inflamed. Egyptian journalist Hani Shukrallah sees these recent protests as evidence that Islamists are trampling the values of freedom, democracy, equality, and fundamental human rights that brought Egypt together for the January 2011 revolution. He sees the Brotherhood moving away from its moderate stance to a more conservative Islamist, authoritarian position. For the time being he says, "the clash of bigotries, ignorance and stupidity is back on center stage".[200]

Other factors besides U.S. security cooperation mitigate renewed Egyptian-Israeli conflict. If he wants to stay in power, Morsi needs to address Egypt's severe economic and social problems. Although unpopular, economic ties with Israel are an important part of Egypt's struggling economy. Open conflict with Israel would likely bring international condemnation and adverse economic impacts on Egypt. There is also little Egyptian capability to challenge Israel through conventional military means. However, if either party terminates the U.S.-Egyptian

---

[198] David A. Bell, "The End of the Beginning" In *Revolution in the Arab World: Tunisia, Egypt, and the Unmaking of an Era*, by Foreign Policy, ed Marc Lynch, B Glasser Susan and Blake Hounshell (n.p.: The Slate Group, A Division of The Washington Post Company, 2011), 216.

[199] Carl von Clausewitz, *On War,* trans. and ed. Michael Howard and Peter Paret. (Princeton: Princeton University Press, 1976), 591-592.

[200] Hani Shukrallah, "Conspiracies of convenience: what's behind the film fracas?" *Al Arabiya News,* September 16, 2012. http://english.alarabiya net/views/2012/09/16/238284 html (accessed September 16, 2012).

security cooperation relationship, there will be little strategic interest for an Islamist Egypt to maintain peace accords with Israel.

At their core, the Brotherhood and Salafist movements seek to unite Muslim countries against Western influence and dominance. Morsi's government will likely strive to renew Egypt's regional leadership role as a counter to Iran. A recent FJP foreign policy statement by Amr Darrag outlines principles for restoring Egypt's rightful place in world affairs. Darrag argues that Egypt will pursue peaceful relations with all countries and base its foreign policy on a foundation of equality and mutual interests, not dependency and domination. This indicates a desire to distance Egypt from U.S. military dependence and influence. Additionally, Darrag stresses the need for broader participation in foreign policy by Egyptian institutions and citizens and the need to support Palestinians in obtaining their legitimate rights.[201] Using the Palestinian issue as a pretext, Sunni Arab Egypt could win broad regional support in a way Shia Persian Iran cannot. With increasing tensions in Gaza and along the Israeli border, Egypt may have to choose between supporting Palestinians or maintaining peace with Israel. Given Egypt's history and current Islamist trends in the region, Morsi is more likely to abrogate the Camp David Accords and a U.S. administration will have limited ability to prevent it.

Conclusion

Several important conclusions emerge from this monograph regarding the Nasser era and the current Muslim Brotherhood era. Although Islamist movements have replaced nationalism as the Arab world's most dynamic force, Nasser left a surviving legacy. He established a military dominated dictatorial political system with the facade of popular politics. He significantly

---

[201] Amr Darrag, "A Revolutionary Foreign Policy" *Foreign Policy,* October 16, 2012. http://www.foreignpolicy.com/articles/2012/10/15/a_revolutionary_foreign_policy?page=0,0 (accessed October 16, 2012). Amr Darrag is chairman of the Foreign Relations Committee of the Freedom and Justice Party and secretary-general of Egypt's Constituent Assembly. Darrag also highlights the need for Morsi's government to help transform the world into a more democratic, humane, equitable and interdependent place by combining Islamic values with principles of the 25 January revolution like freedom, human dignity and social justice.

changed Egyptian society, uprooted the old landed class and foreign community, implemented modest redistribution of property, and extended educational opportunities to all Egyptians. He supported industrialism and gave Egypt sovereignty over its resources. Nasser's foreign policy promoted pan-Arabism, non-alignment, and anti-imperialism. He became a threat to Western interests in the region and a leader in the Arab world: a liberator from colonialism, monarchical rule, and Zionism.

The political triumph of Islamists in general and the Brotherhood specifically is the essential outcome of Egypt's recent revolution. Realizing an exceptional opportunity for political advancement, the Brotherhood supported the overthrow of Mubarak and the transition to democracy. The Brotherhood is an Islamist movement with a long tradition in Egyptian politics and society that was very active during the Nasser era. However, this is the first time Islamist parties have held the preponderance of political power in Egypt.

On the surface, Egypt's revolutions gave hope that freedom, democracy, and improved economic conditions would spread over the country. However, the systemic political, economic, and social problems were just as difficult for the new governments to address as they were for the old regimes. President Morsi has the opportunity to reverse Egypt's systemic problems, but he does not have very much time. The revolutions were about human dignity and justice; however, they were also about the dignity of Egypt taking its rightful place in the region, independent of British, U.S., or Israeli interests. If Morsi's government is not able to address its internal concerns adequately, it may look externally for scapegoats. Based on the systemic tensions in Egypt, the U.S. and Israel are the most likely candidates.

Increasing tension between Israel and a new Egyptian government presents an extraordinary challenge for Western countries. Although the U.S. would like to reduce strategic resources committed to the MENA region, the current political, economic, and social conditions in Egypt and the area in general indicate a need for significant engagement. The recent storming of the U.S. Embassy in Cairo and anti-U.S. protests on 11 September demonstrates the deep resentment felt about U.S. foreign policy. The challenge of managing a new relationship with Egypt is complicated even more by the debt crisis facing the U.S. and the European Union. Declining budgets and increased focus on domestic issues will make it difficult for Western democracies to respond effectively to the new situation in the Arab world. Since the West depends on a stable Middle East for a secure oil market, it must take a new strategic approach to address the Arab revolutions and the conditions that are driving them. This strategy should focus on supporting new democratic-minded civil society movements and peacefully resolving the Israeli-Palestinian conflict. Most importantly, however, the West needs to invest in economic reforms that will allow Arab countries to use their educated and skilled labor force as part of a modern economy.

If current trends continue and Egypt's economic and social conditions are not mitigated through diplomatic and economic engagement, Western countries may resort to military means to prevent or respond to a new crisis in the Sinai region. A major conflict that threatens access to the Suez Canal would generate pressure for U.S. or NATO military intervention. NATO could use military force to separate conventional hostile forces and maintain the sea-lane through the Suez. However, a hostile Egyptian government and populace would likely use unconventional means such as guerrilla forces and terrorist attacks to counter any intervention. Intervention would also inflame other Arab populations and further empower conservative Islamist organizations.

BIBLIOGRAPHY

Achy, Lahcen. "Arab World: To Fight Off Hunger and Food Shortages, Governments Must Plan." *Carnegie Moscow Center.* November 11, 2010. http://carnegie.ru/publications/?fa=41906 (accessed September 25, 2011).

AFP. "Egypt's Islamist-led parliament calls for expulsion of Israeli envoy." *Al Arabiya News.* March 12, 2012. http://english.alarabiya.net/articles/2012/03/12/200287.html (accessed September 2, 2012).

—. "Muslim Brotherhood wins nearly half the seats in the Egyptian parliament." *Al Arabiya News.* January 21, 2012. http://english.alarabiya.net/articles/2012/01/21/189694.html (accessed September 2, 2012).

Aftandilian, Gregory. *Presidential Succession Scenarios in Egypt and Their Impact on U.S.-Egyptian Strategic Relations.* Monograph, Carlisle, PA: Strategic Studies Institute, United States Army War College, September 2011.

Ahram Online. "Relive vote count in 1st round of Egypt presidential race: How Morsi and Shafiq moved on." *Ahram Online.* May 25, 2012. http://english.ahram.org.eg/NewsContent/36/122/42755/Relive-vote-count-in-st-round-of-Egypt-presidentia.aspx (accessed September 16, 2012).

Al Arabiya with Agencies. "Egyptian court suspends Islamists-dominated constitutional assembly." *Al Arabiya News.* April 10, 2012. http://english.alarabiya.net/articles/2012/04/10/206737.html (accessed September 16, 2012).

—. "Egyptians wrap up 2nd round of phased election; Islamists set to dominate." *Al Arabiya.* December 15, 2011. http://english.alarabiya.net/articles/2011/12/15/182796.html (accessed September 6, 2012).

—. "Islamist party wins majority seats in upper house of Egypt's parliament." *Al Arabia News.* February 25, 2012. http://english.alarabiya.net/articles/2012/02/25/196984.html (accessed September 2, 2012).

al-Banna, Hassan. "Jihad." *Young Muslims.* Edited by Prelude Ltd. 1997. http://web.youngmuslims.ca/online_library/books/jihad/ (accessed September 6, 2012).

Anderson, Lisa. "Demystifying the Arab Spring: Parsing the Differences Between Tunisia, Egypt, and Libya." *Foreign Affairs*, May/June 2011: 2-7.

Antle, W. James. "Senate overwhelmingly rejects foreign aid cuts for Egypt, Libya and Pakistan." *The Daily Caller.* September 23, 2012. http://dailycaller.com/2012/09/23/senate-overwhelmingly-rejects-foreign-aid-cuts-for-egypt-libya-and-pakistan/ (accessed September 23, 2012).

Ashour, Omar. "Egypt's Democratic Jihadists?" In *Islamists in a Changing Middle East*, by Foreign Policy, edited by Marc Lynch, 67-69. N.p.: The FP Group, a division of the Washington Post Company, 2012.

Associated Press. "Egypt's president cancels amendments that gave military power, names vice president." *Fox News.* August 12, 2012. http://www.foxnews.com/world/2012/08/12/egypt-president-cancels-amendments-that-gave-military-power-names-vice/#ixzz23Mr373f3 (accessed September 23, 2012).

Ayoob, Mohammed. "The Tyrant is Dead, But What About His Tyranny?" In *Revolution in the Arab World: Tunisia, Egypt, and the Unmaking of an Era*, by Foreign Policy, edited by Marc Lynch, B Glasser Susan and Blake Hounshell, 211-212. N.p.: The Slate Group, A Division of The Washington Post Company, 2011.

Bamyeh, Mohammad. "The Egyptian Revolution: First Impressions from the Field." *Middle East Institute.* February 8, 2011. http://www.mei.nus.edu.sg/blog/country/egypt/the-egyptian-revolution-first-impressions-from-the-field (accessed September 4, 2012).

BBC World Service. *Views of US Continue to Improve in 2011 BBC Country Rating Poll.* Opinion Poll, London: BBC World Service, 2011.

Bell, David A. "The End of the Beginning." In *Revolution in the Arab World: Tunisia, Egypt, and the Unmaking of an Era*, by Foreign Policy, edited by Marc Lynch, B Glasser Susan and Blake Hounshell, 213-217. N.p.: The Slate Group, A Division of The Washington Post Company, 2011.

Blair, Edmund, and Marwa Awad. "Egypt's army faces wrath for delaying civilian rule." *Al Arabiya News.* November 22, 2011. http://english.alarabiya.net/articles/2011/11/22/178548.html (accessed September 2, 2012).

Blumberg, Alex. "Why Egypt's Military Cares About Home Appliances." *National Public Radio.* February 4, 2011. http://www.npr.org/blogs/money/2011/02/10/133501837/why-egypts-military-cares-about-home-appliances (accessed December 13, 2011).

Bohn, Lauren. "Inside Egypt's Salafis." In *Islamists in a Changing Middle East*, by Foreign Policy, edited by Marc Lynch, 73-76. N.p.: The FP Group, a division of the Washington Post Company, 2011.

Botman, Selma. *Egypt from Independence to Revolution, 1919-1952.* Syracuse: Syracuse University Press, 1991.

Bouckaert, Peter. "February 9: Egypt's Foreigner Blame Game." In *Revolution in the Arab World: Tunisia, Egypt, and the Unmaking of an Era*, by Foreign Policy, edited by Marc Lynch, B Glasser Susan and Blake Hounshell, 102-106. N.p.: The Slate Group, A Division of The Washington Post Company, 2011.

Brown, Lester. "The Great Food Crisis of 2011." *Foreign Policy.* January 10, 2011. http://www.foreignpolicy.com/articles/2011/01/10/the_great_food_crisis_of_2011?page=full (accessed September 24, 2011).

—. "This will be the Arab world's next battle." *The Guardian.* April 22, 2011. http://www.guardian.co.uk/commentisfree/2011/apr/22/water-the-next-arab-battle (accessed September 25, 2011).

Cafiero, Giorgio. "Can Egypt Chart Its Own Course?" *Foreign Policy in Focus.* September 17, 2012. http://www.fpif.org/articles/can_egypt_chart_its_own_course (accessed September 30, 2012).

Casey, Mary, and Jennifer Parker. "New Egyptian president looks to reinstate parliament." *Foreign Policy.* July 2, 2012. http://mideast.foreignpolicy.com/posts/2012/07/02/new_egyptian_president_looks_to_reinstate_parliament (accessed July 6, 2012).

Central Intelligence Agency. *World Fact Book.* September 13, 2012. https://www.cia.gov/library/publications/the-world-factbook/geos/eg.html (accessed September 30, 2012).

Clausewitz, Carl von. *On War.* Edited by Michael Howard and Peter Paret. Translated by Michael Howard and Peter Paret. Princeton: Princeton University Press, 1976.

Clinton, Hillary Rodham, and Timothy F. Geithner. "Letter to G8 Ministers on Supporting Arab Spring." *U.S. Department of State.* May 25, 2011. http://translations.state.gov/st/english/texttrans/2011/05/20110525104312su0.936134.html (accessed November 27, 2011).

Clover, Charles, and Roula Khalaf. "Egypt Military Uneasy over Business Ties." *Financial Times.* February 28, 2011. http://www.ft.com/cms/s/0/a301b6ec-435b-11e0-8f0d-00144feabdc0,s01=1.html#axzz1gaRnbMEq (accessed December 13, 2011).

Commodity Online. "Food crisis threatens import dependent Arab nations." *Commodity Online.* January 21, 2011. http://www.commodityonline.com/news/Food-crisis-threatens-import-dependent-Arab-nations-35836-3-1.html (accessed September 24, 2011).

Dabbs, Brian. "Muslim Brotherhood No Threat to Egypt's Israel Policy." *World Politics Review.* July 21, 2011. http://www.worldpoliticsreview.com/articles/9542/muslim-brotherhood-no-threat-to-egypts-israel-policy (accessed September 6, 2012).

Darrag, Amr. "A Revolutionary Foreign Policy." *Foreign Policy.* October 16, 2012. http://www.foreignpolicy.com/articles/2012/10/15/a_revolutionary_foreign_policy?page=0,0 (accessed October 16, 2012).

Egypt.com. "Egypt's MB to play a large economic role, experts claim." *Egypt.com.* August 2, 2011. http://news.egypt.com/english/permalink/26660.html (accessed September 6, 2012).

Elyan, Tamim. "Egyptians angry at film scale U.S. embassy walls." *Reuters.* September 11, 2012. http://www.reuters.com/article/2012/09/11/us-egypt-usa-protest-idUSBRE88A11N20120911 (accessed September 30, 2012).

Fadel, Leila. "Egypt's Muslim Brotherhood forms coalition with liberal party." *The Washington Post.* June 13, 2011. http://www.washingtonpost.com/world/egypts-muslim-brotherhood-forms-coalition-with-liberal-party/2011/06/13/AGQI7OTH_story.html (accessed September 6, 2012).

—. "Muslim Brotherhood asserts its strength in Egypt with challenges to military." *The Washington Post.* March 25, 2012. http://www.washingtonpost.com/world/middle_east/muslim-brotherhood-asserts-its-strength-in-egypt-with-challenges-to-military/2012/03/21/gIQAJ9pmaS_story.html (accessed September 6, 2012).

Fahim, Kareem, and Dina Salah Amer. "Uncertainties Underlie the Celebrations in Cairo." *The New York Times.* June 18, 2012. http://www.nytimes.com/2012/06/19/world/middleeast/uncertainty-underlies-celebrations-in-cairo.html?_r=1&ref=world (accessed July 7, 2012).

Fathi, Yasmine. "A tale of two Egyptian revolutions." *Ahram Online.* July 23, 2012. http://english.ahram.org.eg/NewsContent/1/139/48329/Egypt/-July-Revolution/A-tale-of-two-Egyptian-revolutions.aspx (accessed September 13, 212).

—. "Brotherhood's Morsi promises national 'renaissance' at Alex campaign rally." *Ahram Online.* April 25, 2012. http://english.ahram.org.eg/NewsContent/36/122/40127/Brotherhoods-Morsi-promises-national-renaissance-a.aspx (accessed September 16, 2012).

Feteha, Ahmed. "Egypt cancels gas deal; Israeli minister warns of 'implications' for Camp David Accords." *Ahram Online.* April 23, 2012.

http://english.ahram.org.eg/NewsContent/3/12/39931/Business/Economy/Egypt-cancels-gas-deal;-Israeli-minister-warns-of-.aspx (accessed September 30, 2012).

Foreign Policy. *Revolution in the Arab World: Tunisia, Egypt, and the Unmaking of an Era.* Edited by Marc Lynch, B Glasser Susan and Blake Hounshell. N.p.: The Slate Group, A Division of The Washington Post Company, 2011.

Fouda, Amira. "Muslim Brotherhood conspired with military council to field presidential candidate: former member." *Al Arabiya News.* April 02, 2012. http://english.alarabiya.net/articles/2012/04/02/204903.html (accessed September 16, 2012).

Friedman, Thomas L. "All Together Now." *The New York Times.* August 27, 2011. http://www.nytimes.com/2011/08/28/opinion/sunday/friedman-all-together-now.html (accessed October 5, 2011).

Gaddis, John Lewis. *Surprise, Security, and the American Experience.* Cambridge, MA: Harvard University Press, 2004.

Gordon, Joel. *Nasser's Blessed Movement: Egypt's Free Officers and the July Revolution.* Oxford: Oxford University Press, 1992.

Government Accountability Office. *State and DOD Need to Assess How the Foreign Military Financing Program for Egypt Achieves U.S. Foreign Policy and Security Goals.* Security Assistance, GAO-06-437, Washington D.C.: United States Government Accountability Office, April 2006.

Hamid, Shadi. "Brother Number One." In *Islamists in a Changing Middle East*, by Foreign Policy, edited by Marc Lynch, 98-102. N.p.: The FP Group, a division of the Washington Post Company, 2012.

—. "It Ain't Just a River in Egypt." *Foreign Policy.* July 30, 2012. http://www.foreignpolicy.com/articles/2012/07/30/it_ain_t_just_a_river_in_egypt?page=0,0 (accessed September 30, 2012).

Hanna, Michael Wahid. "Sectarianism Stalks Egypt." In *Islamists in a Changing Middle East*, by Foreign Policy, edited by Marc Lynch, 64-67. N.p.: The FP Group, a division of the Washington Post Company, 2012.

Hounshell, Blake. "February 11: Pharaoh is Dead, Long Live Pharaoh?" In *Revolution in the Arab World: Tunisia, Egypt, and the Unmaking of an Era*, by Foreign Policy, edited by Marc Lynch, B Glasser Susan and Blake Hounshell, 110-114. N.p.: The Slate Group, A Division of The Washington Post Company, 2011.

Ibrahim, Ekram, Zeinab El Gundi, Yasmine Fathi, and Hatem Maher. *Ahram Online Presidential Elections 2012.* April 2, 2012. http://english.ahram.org.eg/UI/Front/Pelections2012.aspx (accessed September 16, 2012).

Ignatius, David. "What Happens When the Arab Spring Turns to Summer?" *Foreign Policy.* April 22, 2011. http://www.foreignpolicy.com/articles/2011/04/22/what_happens_when_the_arab_spring_turns_to_summer (accessed September 28, 2011).

Kaplan, Robert D. "The New Arab World Order." In *Revolution in the Arab World: Tunisia, Egypt, and the Unmaking of an Era*, by Foreign Policy, edited by Marc Lynch, B Glasser Susan and Blake Hounshell, 173-174. N.p.: The Slate Group, A Division of The Washington Post Company, 2011.

Kessler, Oren. "Egypt Islamist vows global caliphate in Jerusalem." *The Jerusalem Post.* May 08, 2012. http://www.jpost.com/MiddleEast/Article.aspx?ID=269074&R=R1 (accessed May 15, 2012).

—. "Sleepless in Jerusalem." *Foreign Policy.* May 24, 2012. http://www.foreignpolicy.com/articles/2012/05/24/the_view_from_jerusalem (accessed May 26, 2012).

KGS NightWatch. "NightWatch for 28 November." *Kforce Government Solutions.* November 28, 2011. http://us1.campaign-archive1.com/?u=817f179ff76c12de2a4e5ba20&id=87daadf9c4&e=30c80bf217 (accessed November 29, 2011).

Khalil, Ashraf. "February 10: We Need to Drag Him From His Palace." In *Revolution in the Arab World: Tunisia, Egypt, and the Unmaking of an Era*, by Foreign Policy, edited by Marc Lynch, B Glasser Susan and Blake Hounshell, 107-109. N.p.: The Slate Group, A Division of The Washington Post Company, 2011.

Khalil, Ashraf. "February 12: After the Party." In *Revolution in the Arab World: Tunisia, Egypt, and the Unmaking of an Era*, by Foreign Policy, edited by Marc Lynch, B Glasser Susan and Blake Hounshell, 115-118. N.p.: The Slate Group, A Division of The Washington Post Company, 2011.

Khalil, Ashraf. "January 25: Tear Gas on the Day of Rage." In *Revolution in the Arab World: Tunisia, Egypt, and the Unmaking of an Era*, by Foreign Policy, edited by Marc Lynch, B Glasser Susan and Blake Hounshell, 73-75. N.p.: The Slate Group, A Division of the Washington Post Company, 2011.

Kirk, Michael. "Revolution in Cairo." *Frontline.* Boston: PBS Distribution (DVD), 2011.

Kirkpatrick, David. "Egypt's New Leader Takes Oath, Promising to Work for Release of Jailed Terrorist." *The New York Times.* June 20, 2012. http://www.nytimes.com/2012/06/30/world/middleeast/morsi-promises-to-work-for-release-of-omar-abdel-rahman.html?_r=1 (accessed September 6, 2012).

Kiser, Robert R. *The History of Peacekeeping in the Sinai Desert 1959-2002.* MMAS Thesis, Fort Leavenworth, KS: U.S Army Command and General Staff College, 2003.

Knickmeyer, Ellen. "The Arab World's Youth Army." In *Revolution in the Arab World: Tunisia, Egypt, and the Unmaking of an Era*, by Foreign Policy, edited by Marc Lynch, B Glasser Susan and Blake Hounshell, 122-126. N.p.: The Slate Group, A Division of The Washington Post Company, 2011.

Lagi, Marco, Karla Z. Bertran, and Yaneer Bar-Yam. "The Food Crises and Political Instability in North Africa and the Middle East." *Cornell University Library.* August 11, 2011. http://arxiv.org/abs/1108.2455 (accessed August 17, 2011).

Lynch, Marc. "Islam Divided Between Salafi-jihad and the Ikhwan." *Studies in Conflict and Terrorism* 33, no. 6 (2010): 467-487.

Lynch, Marc. "Tahrir turning points." In *Islamists in a Changing Middle East*, by Foreign Policy, edited by Marc Lynch, 70-72. N.p.: The FP Group, a division of the Washington Post Company, 2012.

Lynch, Marc. "The Muslim Brotherhood's Presidential Gambit." In *Islamists in a Changing Middle East*, by Foreign Policy, edited by Marc Lynch, 90-92. N.p.: The FP Group, a division of the Washington Post Company, 2012.

Martenson, Chris. "Egypt's Warning: Are you Listening?" *Chris Martenson.Com.* February 9, 2011. http://www.chrismartenson.com/blog/egypts-warning-are-you-listening/52575 (accessed September 24, 2011).

Mazel, Zvi. "Analysis: Brotherhood taking total control of Egypt." *The Jerusalem Post.* August 23, 2012. http://www.jpost.com/MiddleEast/Article.aspx?ID=282258 (accessed September 23, 2012).

McCormick, Ty. "The Arab Recession." *Foreign Policy.* July 22, 2011. http://www.foreignpolicy.com/articles/2011/07/22/the_arab_recession?page=full (accessed September 21, 2011).

Mills, Robin M. "Foreign Policy." *Power Play.* April 27, 2012. http://www.foreignpolicy.com/articles/2012/04/27/power_play (accessed April 28, 2012).

Multinational Force and Observers. *Multinational Force and Observers.* 2012. http://www.mfo.org/index.php (accessed February 13, 2012).

Nasser, Gamal Abdul. *Egypt's Liberation: The Philosophy of the Revolution.* Washington D.C.: Public Affairs Press, 1955.

Office of the Spokesman. "Assistance to Egypt-Fact Sheet." *U.S. Department of State.* May 19, 2011. http://www.state.gov/r/pa/prs/ps/2011/05/163818.htm (accessed November 27, 2011).

Osama, Shams El-Din. *A Military History of Modern Egypt from the Ottoman Conquest to the Ramadan War.* SAMS Monograph, Fort Leavenworth, KS: School of Advanced Military Studies, United States Army Command and General Staff College, 2007.

Perry, Tom. "Egypt's Muslim Brotherhood must face up to historic duty." *Al Arabia News.* May 31, 2012. http://english.alarabiya.net/articles/2012/05/31/217808.html (accessed September 16, 2012).

Pollack, Kenneth M. *Arabs at War: Miliitary Effectiveness, 1948-1991.* Lincoln: University of Nebraska Press, 2002.

Reuters. "Egypt Sinai peacekeepers deny they came under fire." *Reuters.* August 12, 2012. http://www.reuters.com/article/2012/08/12/us-egypt-sinai-attack-idUSBRE87A0MD20120812 (accessed October 5, 2012).

—. "Egypt's new president faces burden of expectation." *Ahram Online.* July 2, 2012. http://english.ahram.org.eg/NewsContent/1/64/46684/Egypt/Politics-/Egypts-new-president-faces-burden-of-expectation.aspx (accessed July 7, 2012).

—. "Newly formed political party will get Egyptian revolution back on track and one day rule the country, says its founder reform leader Mohamed ElBaredei." *ITN Source.* April 28, 2012. http://www.itnsource.com/shotlist/RTV/2012/04/28/RTV1304912/ (accessed September 6, 2012).

—. "Polling stations open in historic Egypt referendum." *ITN Source.* March 20, 2011. http://www.itnsource.com/en/shotlist//RTV/2011/03/20/RTV819711/?s=March+19+2011+referendum+Egypt&st=0&pn=1&v=0 (accessed September 6, 2012).

Richards, Alan, and John Waterbury. *A Political Economy of the Middle East.* Boulder, Colorado: Westview Press, 2008.

Rivlin, Paul. *Arab Economies in the Twenty-First Century.* New York: Cambridge University Press, 2009.

Rodrigue, Jean-Paul. "Straits, Passages and Chokepoints: A Maritime Geostrategy of Petroleum Distribution." *Erudit.* December 2004. http://www.erudit.org/revue/cgq/2004/v48/n135/011797ar.html?lang=en (accessed April 26, 2012).

Rogin, Josh. "Gates and Mullen in close contact with Egyptian military." *Foreign Policy.* February 11, 2011. http://thecable.foreignpolicy.com/posts/2011/02/11/gates_and_mullen_in_close_contact_with_egyptian_military (accessed September 30, 2012).

Rozen, Laura. "Former officials, scholars warned of coming instability in Egypt." *Politico.* January 30, 2011. http://www.politico.com/blogs/laurarozen/0111/They_told_us_Former_officials_scholars_warned_of_coming_instability_in_Egypt.html (accessed July 14, 2012).

Rubin, Barry, ed. *Revolutionaries and Reformers: Contemporary Islamist Movements in the Middle East* . Albany, New York: State University of New York Press, 2003.

Sharp, Jeremy M. *Egypt in Transition.* Report for Congress, Washington D.C.: Congressional Research Service, August 23, 2011.

Shehata, Said. "The misery of Copts in Egypt ." *Ahram Online.* October 2, 2012. http://english.ahram.org.eg/NewsContentP/4/54512/Opinion/The-misery-of-Copts-in-Egypt--.aspx (accessed October 2, 2012).

Shukrallah, Hani. "Conspiracies of convenience: what's behind the film fracas?" *Al Arabiya News.* September 16, 2012. http://english.alarabiya.net/views/2012/09/16/238284.html (accessed September 16, 2012).

Singh, Michael. "What has really changed in the Middle East?" *Foreign Policy.* September 22, 2011. http://shadow.foreignpolicy.com/posts/2011/09/22/what_has_really_changed_in_the_middle_east (accessed September 25, 2011).

Smith, Martin, and Charles M. Sennott. "The Brothers." *Frontline.* Boston: PBS Distribution (DVD), 2011.

Springborg, Robert. "Egypt's cobra and mongoose." In *Islamists in a Changing Middle East*, by Foreign Policy, edited by Marc Lynch, 58-61. N.p.: The FP Group, a division of the Washington Post Company, 2012.

Tal, David. *The 1956 War: Collusion and Rivalry in the Middle East.* Portland, OR: Frank Cass Publishers, 2001.

Terrill, W. Andrew. "Breaking News Analysis: The Future of the U.S. Political and Military Relationship with Egypt." *Strategic Studies Institute, U.S. Army War College.* July 9, 2012. http://www.strategicstudiesinstitute.army.mil/index.cfm/articles/Future-of-the-US-Political-and-Military-Relationship-with-Egypt/2012/07/09 (accessed September 6, 2012).

Terrill, W. Andrew. *The Arab Spring and the Future of U.S. Interests and Cooperative Security in the Arab World.* Opinion Editorial, Carliise, PA: Strategic Studies Institute, United States Army War College, August 2011.

The New York Times. "Muslim Brotherhood (Egypt)." *The New York Times.* Sept 7, 2012. http://topics.nytimes.com/top/reference/timestopics/organizations/m/muslim_brotherhood_egypt/index.html (accessed September 9, 2012).

Topol, Sarah A. "Egypt's Salafi Surge." In *Islamists in a Changing Middle East*, by Foreign Policy, edited by Marc Lynch, 83-85. N.p.: The FP Group, a division of the Washington Post Company, 2012.

Toronto, Nathan. *Active Inaction: Interagency Security Assistance to Egypt.* Interagency Occasional Paper, Fort Leavenworth, Kansas: CGSC Foundation Press, No. 6, November 2011.

—. "Egypt's 'Coup-volution'." *Middle East Insights*, February 16, 2011.

Trager, Eric. "Egypt's Triangular Power Struggle." *The Washington Institute.* July 22, 2011. http://www.washingtoninstitute.org/policy-analysis/view/egypts-triangular-power-struggle (accessed September 6, 2012).

USAID. "USAID Country Page-Egypt." *USAID.* August 5, 2011. http://www.usaid.gov/locations/middle_east/countries/egypt/ (accessed November 27, 2011).

Varble, Derek. *The Suez Crisis 1956.* Oxford: Osprey Publishing Limited, 2003.

Vidino, Lorenzo. *The New Muslim Brotherhood in the West.* New York: Columbia University Press, 2010.

Vogelsang, Susan S. *U.S.-Egypt Security Cooperation after Egypt's January 2011 Revolution.* Monograph, Fort Leavenworth, KS: School of Advanced Military Studies, United States Army Command and General Staff College, 2011.

Wolman, David. "The Instigators." *The Atavist.* no. 4. Brooklyn, New York: Atavist Inc., April/May 2011.

Wood, David. "At Risk in Egypt's Turmoil: U.S. Military Access to the Middle East." *Politics Daily.* 2011. http://www.politicsdaily.com/2011/02/05/at-risk-in-egypts-turmoil-u-s-military-access-to-the-middle-e/ (accessed September 6, 2012).

Zedan, David. "Radical Islam in Egypt." In *Revolutionaries and Reformers: Contemporary Islamist Movements in the Middle East*, edited by Barry Rubin, 11-22. Albany: State University of New York, 2003.